TEAM UP

TEAM UP

How Collaboration Powers Superhero Comics

MARIE SARTAIN

University Press of Mississippi / Jackson

The University Press of Mississippi is the scholarly publishing agency of
the Mississippi Institutions of Higher Learning: Alcorn State University,
Delta State University, Jackson State University, Mississippi State University,
Mississippi University for Women, Mississippi Valley State University,
University of Mississippi, and University of Southern Mississippi.

www.upress.state.ms.us

The University Press of Mississippi is a member
of the Association of University Presses.

Publisher: University Press of Mississippi, Jackson, USA
Authorised GPSR Safety Representative: Easy Access System Europe -
Mustamäe tee 50, 10621 Tallinn, Estonia, gpsr.requests@easproject.com

Library of Congress Cataloging-in-Publication Data

Names: Sartain, Marie author
Title: Team up : how collaboration powers superhero comics / Marie Sartain.
Description: Jackson : University Press of Mississippi, 2026. | Includes
bibliographical references and index.
Identifiers: LCCN 2025045311 (print) | LCCN 2025045312 (ebook) | ISBN
9781496860972 hardback | ISBN 9781496860989 trade paperback | ISBN
9781496860996 epub | ISBN 9781496861009 epub | ISBN 9781496861016 pdf |
ISBN 9781496861023 pdf
Subjects: LCSH: Marvel Comics Group | DC Comics, Inc | Superheroes—Comic
books, strips, etc. | Comics artists | Authorship—Collaboration |
Artistic collaboration
Classification: LCC PN6725 .S3633 2026 (print) | LCC PN6725 (ebook)
LC record available at https://lccn.loc.gov/2025045311
LC ebook record available at https://lccn.loc.gov/2025045312

British Library Cataloging-in-Publication Data available

To Steven, whose encouragement made this book possible.

CONTENTS

INTRODUCTION

Creating a mainstream superhero comic is, by the industry's very nature, a complicated exercise. While independent (or "indie") comic books and graphic novels are often written and drawn by a single person, such undertakings can take months if not years. Mainstream comics, however, operate under much faster deadlines, requiring the creation of plot, dialogue, penciling, inking, and coloring every single month. Because it would be nearly impossible for one person to meet such demands, it's unsurprising that most—if not all—modern superhero comics are group endeavors. A glance at any modern comic book issue, with its lists of contributing writers and artists, seems to make this as plain as day.

However, that's only the beginning of how collaboration works when it comes to creating these comic books. If you look further, beyond the neat list of job titles on the cover, the reality of how these stories are created becomes far more complicated. A contributor's title may not fully encapsulate what they brought to the table. The company may have exerted its influence as copyright holder, limiting or directing the decisions of these individual creators in the pursuit of the company's goals. The distinction between consumer and creator may begin to blur. Just as the medium of comics is a balancing act of verbal storytelling and visual art, a comic book is the fusion of ideas and contributions from multiple sources.

But while this reality is common knowledge among creators, fans, and scholars, there is very little actually written about the subject of collaboration and its effects upon these comics as an industry and as a subgenre. In both public and academic discussion of superhero comics, the power of collaboration is often left unsaid or under-stated. The comic book writer is treated as the primary creative force behind these beloved characters. When readers discuss superheroes, they describe creative decisions like they were the sole decision of a given issue's writer, as if the artists who produced its colorful visual illustrations were nothing but extensions of that writer's vision.

This conflation is unfortunate but perhaps expected. In the United States in particular, there is a social valuation of the pioneering spirit, self-sufficiency, and fierce creative independence. Americans, as the received wisdom tells us, should be able to pursue their visions alone. We initially learn about Thomas Edison as a trailblazing engineer who had over a thousand patents, not the team of engineering geniuses who worked in Edison's laboratories to churn out these groundbreaking inventions. As a result, we are prone to believe what Jack Stillinger calls "the myth of the solitary genius," or the idea of a genius who works alone, without the help or influence of others. But the myth of the solitary genius is just that: a myth. Even the most brilliant, famous creators had their work shaped by others, whose input went unacknowledged. If this is the case for works that are commonly considered single-author texts—for example, Stillinger points the poetry of John Keats and William Wordsworth—then it is certainly not the case in explicitly collaborative projects like superhero comics.

This myth is not just present in popular discourse. The study of comics as a literary and artistic medium also encounters such problems. While many comics scholars note that the visual image is an integral part of comics and separates comics from other forms of writing (Groensteen 8), and that the traditional notion of authorship is troubled by the presence of multiple creative forces in comics (Bredehoft 98), these same scholars often do so only in passing, focusing more on the more traditional literary aspects of comics rather than the effects of multimodal cocreation on the medium as a whole.

For example, the most thorough analysis of the impact of collaboration in comics creation before this book has been done by Thomas A. Bredehoft, who explores authorial positions in autobiographical graphic novels written by Henry Pekar and illustrated by various artists. But even though Bredehoft initially states that privileging the writer as the sole author is antithetical to comics as a medium (98), he does not carry this sentiment into his analytical practice. Although he acknowledges that the series of artists create wide variances in the finished products (98) and suggests that the creation of a work's visual style is to some extent a matter of authorship (100), Bredehoft does not treat the visual artists as Pekar's creative equals. Instead, Bredehoft refers to Pekar as a casting director for the artists who work on "his" (101)—not "their"—comics; any visual differences, in Bredehoft's view, are heteroglossic elements that Pekar purposefully employs, not instances in which the artists are contributing their own vision to the collaborative project. In Bredehoft's view, the artists are not cocreators, but "Pekar's Artists" (100).

If scholars have been reticent to study the role of collaboration of writers and artists in the comic-as-text, they have been even less eager to explore the impact of corporate agendas and fan participation, which are driving forces that indelibly influence the creation of mainstream comics. Thus, the effects of collaborative authorship in mainstream comics—both in terms of collaborations between writers and artists, and of the influence corporate copyright holders and fans exert on the larger storytelling enterprise—have gone largely unexplored until quite recently.

What does it mean if our understanding of comic books does not account for their collaborative creation? First, treating these stories as the writer's solitary enterprise ignores the contributions made by others. It devalues those contributors' work, their long hours of effort and toil, and credits it to others, denying these people the proper attribution for their labor. Second, the valorization of this myth prevents us from better understanding how these stories work—how they are produced and received.

This book fills this gap by examining the role of collaboration in the American superhero comics industry on both the individual and mass scale. By taking a broad definition of multiple authorship—recognizing the influence of artists, corporate copyright holders, and participatory fandoms on the creative process—I argue that collaborative authorship powers superhero comics on every level, from its creation process to its reception. In doing so, I seek to shift our understanding of superhero comics away from the "myth of the solitary genius" (Stillinger 22) toward one that embraces collaborative authorship as a foundational aspect of the genre, and to a larger extent the comics industry in general.

This book is divided into four chapters. The first two are focused on the collaboration process within individual collaborative teams, while the final two examine collaborations that take place on a mass scale. In chapter 1, "Who Cowrote the *Watchmen*?: Alan Moore, Multiple Authorship, and Convergence Culture," I examine the creation process of *Watchmen* and how its various collaborative partners approached its postproduction transformation into a graphic novel. Despite the work's reputation as Alan Moore's magnum opus, I not only demonstrate that the limited series was fundamentally shaped by the influence of DC Comics editors, but that the specific circumstances of the series' creation created increased opportunities for penciler-inker Dave Gibbons to provide authorial input. I also discuss how the traditional division of roles may have influenced the individual reactions Moore and his creative partners had when DC transformed the limited series into a continuously published trade paperback, thus denying them eventual copyright ownership. Through this examination, I show 1) that the works of Alan Moore—one of superhero comics' greatest writers—were the product of collaborative authorship, 2) that strict titles used for collaborators' roles in comics (e.g., writer, artist, etc.) may belie the true extent to which a collaborator may contribute to the work as a whole, and 3) that these titles and their relevant levels of prestige might affect a collaborator's level of personal connection to their work, thereby possibly alienating them from their own creations.

In chapter 2, "Marvel Madness: Stan Lee and the 'Marvel Method,'" I address claims that Stan Lee, who is credited with the creation of numerous iconic Marvel Comics characters, took credit for the contributions of others through his popularization of the production process now known as the "Marvel Method." Using archival evidence found in the Stan Lee Papers at University of Wyoming's American Heritage Center, I attempt to determine the extent to which artists working with Stan Lee and his "Marvel Method" acted as coauthors. Through this, I model the archival work that may be required to determine the true extent of coauthorship in comics.

Beginning with chapter 3, "Which Earth is This Again?: The Retcon vs. the Multiverse," this book moves away from individual examples of multiple authorship to conceptualize how collaborative writing functions on a larger scale in superhero comics. This chapter conceives the creative teams who successively write about particular superheroes as participants in a continuous long-term collaborative project that must balance previously published stories with the desire to create new, innovative stories. Following an explanation of how continuity developed as an important aspect of superhero comics, I focus on two techniques used to preserve continuity while allowing for creative experimentation: retroactive continuity changes (also known as retcons) and multiverses. I argue that retcons, which I separate into two broad categorizations ("soft" and "hard"), allow the current creative team to either alter or erase past continuity in order to enable their own narrative visions, while multiverses allow for multiple conflicting storylines to exist simultaneously without altering past continuity. I discuss the specific benefits and disadvantages of each in terms of maintaining the viability of long-term collaborative storytelling in superhero comics.

In my final chapter, "Sharing the Sandbox: Corporate Interests and Fandoms," I explore how fans of superhero comics act not only as consumers, but as cocreators of superhero mythos. Beginning with how the comics industry encouraged the formation of a highly participatory fandom, I discuss the relationship fans of superhero comics have with their source materials. Using an expanded version the industry's "sandbox" metaphor, I argue that this history has led to a fandom that feels a particular sense of ownership over their source texts and thus have unique tensions with corporate copyright owners. I then transition to discussions of how fan communities transform these published works through the formation of creative interpretations known as "headcanons," fandom community-held unofficial canon or "fanon," and the creation of fanworks. I argue that these interpretive practices both alter fan reception and expand the boundaries of the official canon, thus transforming these fans into coauthors of the text.

TEAM UP

CHAPTER 1

WHO COWROTE THE *WATCHMEN?*
Alan Moore, Multiple Authorship, and Convergence Culture

Introduction

When discussing the history of American superhero comics, *Watchmen* is an evitable topic. In an environment in which super-heroes were (and arguably still are) "the defining force within the American comic book marketplace, as well as the basis of the most common prejudice surrounding the medium" (Goggin and Hassler-Forest 3) that comics are solely for children's entertain-ment, the 1985–86 limited series by DC Comics upended these expectations. *Watchmen*'s mature storytelling, featuring deeply flawed characters and Cold War existential terror, paired with Frank Miller, Klaus Janson, and Lynn Varley's 1986 *The Dark Knight Returns* (also published by DC), has caused many creators, fans, and scholars to see 1986 as "the year that comics grew up" (Marz), or the point when general and critical audiences came to recog-nize the potential of mainstream comics to be a literary genre in its own right. Because of his role as writer for *Watchmen* among other lauded projects, Alan Moore has earned the reputation as one of the greatest writers in mainstream comics. When he announced his retirement in July 2019 (Thielman), Moore's contributions to this medium were deservedly lauded.

However, it is also vital to recognize the ways in which these achievements were supported by the officially unrecognized contributions of others. Although *Watchmen* is considered one of the greatest graphic novels of the twentieth century for both its iconoclastic writing and innovative use of artwork, literary scholarship and fandom both treat *Watchmen* as solely Alan Moore's magnum opus. But even though Moore is well-known for writing extremely thorough scripts for comics—the one for the first issue of *Watchmen* was a full ninety-one pages of "dense typescript" (Gibbons)—to suggest that *Watchmen* sprang, Athena-like, from Moore's mind without creative influence from others does not reflect the full circumstances that led to this seminal work of visual narrative. In fact, an examination of this series' creation process reveals that coauthorship and corporate/artist convergence shaped the creation and afterlife of *Watchmen* and highlights both the ways in which outside forces—particularly illustrator Dave Gibbons and publisher DC Comics—acted as unequal partners in the creative process as well as the effect of these relationships on the reception and continued use of *Watchmen* as an intellectual property.

Preproduction

From the project's earliest stages, the editors at DC were active in shaping the development of *Watchmen* to better suit the company's own corporate agenda. The original idea that would eventually become *Watchmen* was first put forth by DC Editor Dick Giordano, who approached Moore, then an up-and-coming comics writer who had achieved some success writing short comics for DC's *AD 2000* (Gibbons 27). Giordano proposed revamping the characters DC had purchased from the now-defunct Charlton Comics in 1983 (Gibbons 29) such as the Question, Captain Atom, and the Blue Beetle.[1] After the first of what would be many long phone conversations between Dave Gibbons and Moore, Gibbons told Giordano—who had been executive editor at Charlton Comics in the 1960s (Moore et al., *Watchmen: The Annotated Edition* 6)—that Moore wanted him to be the illustrator for *Watchmen*. Giordano reportedly gave him the job on the spot (Gibbons 28). John Higgins was signed on as colorist.

However, before the project could take off, there was a dramatic change in plans: after receiving Moore's initial story pitch, the DC editors revoked permission to use the characters purchased from Charlton Comics in *Watchmen*.

It is at this junction that we see the first hints of convergence culture, a media culture in which "multiple media systems coexist and where media content flows fluidly across them . . . an ongoing process or series of intersections between different media systems" (Jenkins, *Convergence Culture* 282). Although they work together to create a finished and marketable product, comics publishers like DC and the creative talent who work with their characters—writers, pencilers, inkers, colorists, letterers, etc.—operate under differing and at times opposing sets of values and priorities. On one hand, individual creators are allowed by DC to briefly use the company's toys, and these creators have full awareness of the brevity of their tenure. Therefore, these creators are strongly motivated to make their work different from anything that has come before so that their work becomes a memorable part of a character's sometimes decades-long history. On the other hand, companies like DC have every reason to *not* let every creator make large changes at will, as such disruptions have a larger-than-zero possibility to turn away readers who were once loyal customers. Therefore, dramatic and permanent changes in character and story are for the most part to be avoided at all costs, or at least not without heavy vetting. While comic book publishers have been known to make changes for shock value—for example, in 1992 DC (briefly) killed off one of its powerhouse characters in the *Death of Superman* crossover event—such radical instances are notable events that often require months of planning and coordination between editors in charge of various properties, only to be eventually reversed in an equally planned-out return.[2] In order to protect their future as a company, mainstream comic book publishers like DC both set the rules by which creators must work and may revoke the privilege of using their products at any time to preserve the long-term marketability of their intellectual property.

Such was the case with Moore's planned usage of Charlton superheroes. DC partially reversed its proposal when it was discovered that this limited series would kill off these relatively family friendly characters or transform them into rapists, serial killers, and/or perpetrators of genocide. Though character resurrections—and often with a change of heart accompanying them—are a common occurrence in comics, the memory of comic book fans can be long. Regular readers of DC's comics, it was feared, might find it difficult to disassociate these characters from their extremely violent and iconoclastic *Watchmen* versions for years to come, directly contraindicating DC's desire to utilize their newly purchased assets. This, it was decided, was too much potential collateral damage for a series that would be on the stands for less than a year, with the expectation of never being published again. Instead, while *Watchmen* was allowed to continue development as a series, it was forbidden to use any of DC's established characters, including those from Charlton Comics (Gibbons 29).

When this pronouncement was made, it was at first a major derailment. Moore, who had until then only worked on short pieces for DC, initially balked. In a later interview with Jon B. Cooke for *Comic Book Artist*, Moore said when Giordano told him to use other characters, he feared that the impact of *Watchmen* as a whole would be lessened. Because his premise had been to use known characters in a completely unfamiliar way, "I didn't think we could do the book with simply characters that were made up, because I thought that would lose all of the emotional resonance those characters had for the readers, which I thought was an important part of the book" (Moore et al., *Watchmen: The Annotated Edition* 29; Cooke). Now, instead of being able to rely on the decades of familiarity Charlton's characters had built up, Moore was asked to build this pathos from scratch. In order to recreate the series' intended effect, *Watchmen* needed to be quickly populated with a host of characters who could command the same emotional effect without infringing on DC's existing properties.

While it was initially a stumbling block instituted for purely financial reasons, this decision forced Moore and Gibbons to create the completely new characters we recognize today and propelled the series towards its current status as an independent graphic narrative. Rather than relying on Charlton creations, which were themselves meant to be close-but-not-quite copies of more famous DC stars, Moore and Gibbons found themselves with more creative freedom. As Dave Gibbons recounts regarding this stage, "[w]e could now create our own embodiments of these basic types, but fine-tune them to our own sensibilities" (29). They could instead draw inspiration from the entire genre of superhero comics—ranging from traditional sources like Will Eisner and Steve Ditko to *Mad*'s 1953 parody "Superduperman" (Moore et al., *Watchmen: The Annotated Edition* 7)—and provide a unique critique by blending characteristics of entire subclasses of superheroes. For example, the *Watchmen* character Nite Owl II, alias Daniel Dreiburg, has features of both DC's Bruce Wayne aka Batman—an animal-themed, gadget-heavy detective who uses his inherited wealth to fund his one-man war on crime—and Charlton Comics' Ted Kord alias Blue Beetle II, who was also much more reliant on self-made gadgets than his predecessor. Similarly, Dr. Manhattan, Moore and Gibson's substitute for Charlton's Captain Atom, who was given his powers by being exposed to an exploding nuclear warhead in space ("Captain Atom [Allen Adam] [Character]"), is the one superpowered being in the *Watchmen* universe and has clear parallels to both the nuclear arms race and the almost religious treatment of DC's overly powered Superman.[3]

In addition to forcing Moore to adapt his *Watchmen* proposal to star original superheroes, this limitation mandated by DC also provided the initial opportunity for increased author collaboration between Moore and Gibbons. Although Moore is officially designated the writer of *Watchmen*, in several instances Gibbons was an active participant in shaping the new cast of characters. While the two were trying to quickly come up with original creations to replace the intended Charlton characters, Gibbons was given a more involved role in their design than would have previously been possible. Rather than drawing Charlton characters in his own style as he would have under Moore's initial proposal, Gibbons took this opening to create characters who were designed "to be individuals, more like the near-caricatures common in European comics, rather than the square-jawed variations of a theme of most American comics" (Gibbons 45), subtly setting itself apart from the American superhero genre that *Watchmen* criticizes. Gibbons also suggested the name of a superhero he made up when he was fourteen: Night Owl, which Moore changed to Nite Owl in order to use what Moore called the "American" spelling (Gibbons 36).

Writing the Watchmen

Once its roster of original characters was approved by DC Comics, the actual creation of *Watchmen* began. In normal circumstances, the comics creation process was and still is a very streamlined process. In a standard production, the editor and writer will discuss the story for the issue; if the basic plot has not been preapproved like the *Watchmen* series, the writer will have to produce a "pitch" to the editor (Bendis 22). The writer then writes a script describing the action and dialogue, and may give suggestions for panel layouts and compositions. The writer then sends the script to the editor for their approval; as the content of the script was already discussed, there should be little need to make major changes. Once the editor goes over the script, it is traditionally given to the penciler, who then draws the comic using pencil (O'Neil 22); hence the title. The editor approves the penciled comic before handing it off to the inker, who goes over the penciler's work in black ink using various tools like brushes, markers, and pens.[4] Copies of the inked lines would then be given, again by the editor, to the colorist so they could select the colors from a company's predetermined set and use markers and/or written notes to show which colors should be applied, and to the letterer, who applies dialogue bubbles and narration boxes and hand-writes the dialogue onto the page. Once the color guides and line art (now with lettering) are edited, they are sent to the press, where the printers create the comic in its finished form (Bendis 22–44; Gibbons 65; see table 1).

As can be seen from this brief description, this process, which was developed by the comics industry to maximize production speeds, also creates both an omnipresent editorial power and isolated creative powers. At all stages of production, the editor(s) may halt any creative decisions they disagree with; only once a new version of the issue is approved by the editor can it go further down the production line. Although the sign of a good editor, both inside and outside of comics publishing, is that the effect of their guiding hand on the finished product is invisible to the reader, the power of the editor is nonetheless apparent at every step of mainstream comics creation.

Additionally, because the editor is responsible for sending the issue to the next stage of the creative team, the traditional process isolates the artistic contributors from each other. In the traditional procedure, all creative members of the team only need to interact with the editor to perform their jobs. Nowhere in the chain of creative custody must writer, penciler, inker, letterer, or colorist speak with one another. While it was not unheard of for writers and pencilers to send notes to the colorist, usually concerning intended effect or notes about the plot not evident solely in the linework, these were often in outside-of-the-margin scribbles (J. Lee), not in extensive or direct communications. While this likely makes it easier for the editor to track the comic's progress and to manage its development, this also makes it difficult for the individual members of the team to form creative collaborations outside of those with editorial powers.

The creation process for *Watchmen*, however, was different from the typical editor-managed procedure. While Dick Giordano was working for DC Comics in the United States, Moore (the writer), Gibbons (who acted as penciler, inker, and letterer), and Higgins (the colorist) were all living and working across the Atlantic, mere hours from each other in England. In the days before email or faxing were commonplace, communications with DC Comics headquarters regarding *Watchmen* production would have needed to be sent and received via one of two options: posted mail, requiring the time for transatlantic turnaround, or Datapost, which would take between one and two days to arrive and had an attached fee for this expedited convenience (Gibbons 65, 70). Requiring editorial approval for each step would hence have cost DC considerable amounts of time, money, or both. Also, Moore had proven himself a capable writer in other projects and "needed no direction and very little editing—really only for typos" (Gibbons 65). The editors at DC Comics seem to therefore have been amenable to granting the *Watchmen* team more creative independence. Although Moore has been publicly tight-lipped about the works he created for DC Comics in recent decades for reasons I will cover later in this chapter, Gibbons, and to a lesser extent Higgins, have been forthcoming regarding their collaborative process.

First, Moore and Gibbons would discuss the upcoming issue via telephone. Moore would have the issue mostly planned in his mind, but Gibbons claims that he would frequently provide suggestions. This conversation would often devolve into wider conversations regarding politics, pop culture, and childhood remembrances, and could last as long as four hours (Gibbons 65). Then Moore would write the issue's script. Often aspects of these extraneous conversation topics found their way into the issue (Gibbons 65), in both the small ways in which American society would have been affected by the presence superheroes—e.g., variations in fashion and technology that contribute to the aesthetics of *Watchmen*—as well as ideas (which I will discuss later) that would eventually become major elements of the plot.

Once Gibbons received the script, which would be unusually lengthy and dense for the industry—1,043 pages of typewritten script for a finished product of 340 pages, with the longest script (for #7) taking up 111 pages (Moore et al., *Watchmen: The Annotated Edition* 7)—he would read through the script, using highlighters to mark important parts of a script that normally contained few paragraph breaks. Gibbons would map out the twenty-eight-page issue using thumbnail sketches to determine panel layout and composition. For the first few issues, Gibbons sent this "issue map" (Gibbons 70) to Moore for his approval, but as production picked up, this practice fell to the wayside. Once the issue map was drawn full-size in blue pencil, Gibbons would then pencil and ink lettering before inking his drawings.[5] The page would then be cleaned of any stray marks, and Gibbons would make "'insurance' copies at [a] local copy store" (Gibbons 70) before sending the inked and lettered art to DC Comics in New York via Datapost. The supplemental material found at the end of each issue would arrive separately from the main script, which Gibbons would illustrate (Gibbons 76).

At this point, Higgins would receive the lettered line art and confer with Moore and Gibbons about coloring ideas (Gibbons 70). Gibbons claims credit for *Watchmen*'s heavy usage of secondary colors—green, orange, and purple—to reflect the moralities depicted, which are muddier than those in more traditional superhero comics, which work more in the primary colors of red, yellow, and blue (see, for example, Superman's costume [Gibbons 70]). In his reminiscences of creating *Watchmen*, Higgins says that in these conversations Gibbons and Moore "might have color suggestions for something specific in a chapter, such as a red, flashing neon sign, so I had to work out how to incorporate those color ideas into what I did in each issue" (Gibbons 166). Taking these suggestions under advisement, Higgins would paint over Gibbons's linework in watercolor, "then marked the equivalent printing ink combination for each color" (Gibbons 171). For example, Rorschach's iconic brown overcoat would be labeled Y3M2C1. Higgins would then create the issue cover by painting over Gibbons's blue pencil drawings with gouache and acrylic paint (Gibbons 76). Once Higgins had finished, the issue would be sent to the printers, where his colored page "would be sent to hand separators[,] who would do up to twelve separate acetate overlays for each page to create a four-color effect. Each overlay representation a 25%, 50%, 75% or solid tone of each of the printing colors: cyan, magenta, yellow" (Gibbons 171), at which point the issue would be ready for sale.

From this summary of the creative process, we can see the ways in which the creation process of *Watchmen* displayed much higher levels of creative collaboration than typically seen in its other DC comics from the same period. Unlike other ongoing DC projects—including *Swamp Thing* and *Batman: The Killing Joke*, both of which Moore was working on at the same time as *Watchmen* (Gibbons 124)—Moore, Gibbons, and Higgins were given staggeringly greater amounts of creative independence in making *Watchmen*. If Gibbons's account, which was approved and published by DC, is to be believed, then Dick Giordano and other DC representatives did not see the development of each issue until they received Gibbons's inked and lettered line art, skipping at least three points which would have required editorial approval in DC's normal processes. It also appears that the three creators were given little feedback regarding the project's course, as Gibbons was unaware of the limited series' success until he and Moore were given a royal treatment during a rare trip to DC's New York offices (Gibbons 118). Rather than being actively managed by Giordano and the rest of DC, Gibbons claims that "[e]verything would go to press virtually untouched, our collective vision left intact. DC's editorial role was largely confined to traffic management, although their design department, in the person of Richard Bruning and Julia Sabbagh, worked closely with me to sharpen design sketches and layouts and bring them to print-ready finish" for promotional materials (Gibbons 65). Rather than being micromanaged by DC editors, the *Watchmen* creative team, it seems, were expected to watch themselves.

Perhaps in order to make up for this lack of DC oversight, Moore, Gibbons, and Higgins naturally formed a more interactive creative collective. Throughout the entire process, writer, line artist/letterer, and colorist were talking with each other, causing a blurring of traditional roles. This blurring can particularly be seen in the contributions of Gibbons to the making of *Watchmen* both on and off the page.

While Moore organized the plot of *Watchmen* as well as most of its twists and turns, in their prescript phone calls Gibbons made suggestions that eventually became some of the most memorable elements of *Watchmen*'s characters and plot. As mentioned earlier in the chapter, Gibbons and Moore used an adapted version of Night Owl, a superhero Gibbons created in his adolescence, to create Nite Owl II. Gibbons also suggested adding a smiley face pin to the Comedian in order to soften his appearance (Gibbons 45); this led to the adoption of the blood-stained smiley face, an image so integral to the aesthetics and tone of *Watchmen* that a magnified version became the project's cover when it was collected into a graphic novel (Moore et al., *Watchmen*).

Furthermore, while they were discussing the ways in which the world of *Watchmen* would have been affected by the presence of actual superheroes, Gibbons mentioned that in such a world the appeal of superhero comics—long a major sector of mainstream comics publishing in our world—would have quickly gone out of fashion, as "a world with real super heroes would have no need of them in comics" (Gibbons 36), suggesting that pirate comics might be the more popular genre there. Moore took this comment, which Gibbons characterizes as a "small, throwaway idea" (Gibbons 36), to create *Tales of the Black Freighter*, a popular pirate comic read by local teenager Bernie throughout the series. The story "Marooned," which the reader is shown small 1–2 panel snippets, acts as a subplot that is woven through the main narrative in *Watchmen*. Through this interweaving, which Leslie Klinger calls ironic simultaneous narrative (Moore et al., *Watchmen: The Annotated Edition* 11), the comic-within-a-comic acts as both resonance and commentary for the rest of the series.

During the production itself, Gibbons also significantly helped create the resolution of one of *Watchmen*'s pivotal subplots: Dr. Manhattan's sojourn to Mars and his eventual decision to return. For the creation of issue 4, when Dr. Manhattan contemplates his sudden escape from a cancer-creation scare on Earth to Mars, Gibbons used a copy of *The Grand Tour: A Traveler's Guide to the Solar System* that he found in his local library to identify interesting geographical features to use for the story; in the penultimate panel, Dr. Manhattan watches a meteor shower from above the Nodus Gordii Mountains (Moore et al., *Watchmen* 4.28.5), which Gibbons later learned meant "Gordian Knot," the name of the lock company in *Watchmen* and a reference to Adrian Veidt, aka Ozymandias's, historical idol, Alexander the Great (Gibbons 204).[6] Later, in issue 9, when Laurie Juspeczyk (alias Silk Spectre II) and Dr. Manhattan debate whether Manhattan should save the Earth, he lands his glass clockwork castle inside another landmark Gibbons had found: the Galle, more popularly known as the "smiley face" crater (Moore et al., *Watchmen* 9.27.1–2; *Planetary Names: Crater, Craters: Galle on Mars*). Though initially unplanned—Gibbons himself says it seems too coincidental to have been as unplanned as it truly was (Gibbons 204)—the inclusion of the Galle crater serves as a symbolic and tacit proof of Dr. Manhattan's final conclusion that rather than human life being pointless and unworthy of saving (Moore et al., *Watchmen* 9.10.6–7, 9.12.9), "to distill so ***specific*** a form from that chaos of ***improbability***, like turning ***air*** into ***gold*** . . . ***that*** is the crowning ***unlikelihood***. The thermodynamic ***miracle***" (Moore et al., *Watchmen* 9.27.1, emphasis original). In a world of terror both existential and nuclear, the utilization of this image Gibbons happened to find in a local library book suggests that not only does the universe have the capacity to create order from chaos but it is one that may even be benevolent.[7] Regardless of whether our own world is "a clock without a craftsman" (Moore et al., *Watchmen* 4.28.1), the world of *Watchmen* shows the unmistakable fingerprints of both Moore and Gibbons.

In addition to the plot and design elements that Gibbons encouraged Moore to incorporate into the world of *Watchmen* are the extra duties Gibbons performed in its production. While Gibbons is only officially credited for *Watchmen*'s line art and lettering, he also took on a number of responsibilities traditionally associated with the editor. While much more informal than normal editor/writer prescript conferences, the phone conversations Gibbons had with Moore served the same purpose of helping to shape the official writer's ideas into a usable format. Gibbons also copyedited Moore's writing, mostly during the lettering stage, and approved of Higgin's color choices before sending it to the printers (Gibbons 65). If, as Jack Stillinger suggests, editors and copyeditors function as collaborative authors, then Gibbons surely meets the measure (Stillinger 50). Although it is possible that Gibbons could be overstating his role in bringing *Watchmen* to its final form, in the absence of a constant editorial presence in the shape of Dick Giordano and the rest of DC, Gibbons inhabited this multiheaded role of artist and editor.

Postproduction Afterlife: Rights and Creative Control

Even while the series was in progress, it was clear that *Watchmen* was different than anything that had come before it. Taken together, the publication of *Watchmen*, *The Dark Knight Returns*, and Art Spiegelman's graphic memoir *Maus: A Survivor's Tale* seemed to suggest a touchstone moment in the trajectory of visual narrative; although all three of these projects were being created separately and only happened to be published in such close proximity to each other, the three works were taken by fans and critics to be "part of the same adultification of a previously juvenile medium" (Gibbons

240). *Watchmen*, it was felt, was a cultural and literary touchstone, one that would forever change the landscape of mainstream comics; this idea remains in many comics histories today.

This sense of sea change can also be seen in the postpublication afterlife of *Watchmen*, particularly in the reaction by DC Comics. Dick Giordano and the rest of DC Comics had granted Moore, Gibbons, and Higgins more or less total creative control during the creation of *Watchmen*, but this attitude changed upon the series' completion. Although the creative talent was too mired in Watchmen's creation to be paying attention to its reception, the DC home office had taken notice. Eager to take advantage of this opportunity, DC created lines of authorized *Watchmen* merchandise. The involvement of the creative team in this stage varied. Although Moore gave extensive input for tie-in roleplaying games by Mayfair Games that incorporated unused covers and illustrations that Gibbons had previously created for the series (Gibbons 243), they were not invited to give their opinions regarding creation and sale of other merchandise such as $1 smiley-face badges (Gibbons 243). It was, hindsight shows, the beginning of the end of *Watchmen* as a product created without corporate control.

With such a reassertion of creative control over *Watchmen* came the reintroduction of the mainstream comic industry's status quo and its inherent inequities. While the current company–creator arrangement in mainstream comic publishing typically allows for the creation of a mind-boggling amount of content per year and a resulting continuous flow of profits, this arrangement has an entrenched balance of power. Although mainstream comics companies are reliant on enthusiastic and truly creative talent to publish desirable content, said talented individuals must follow these companies' dictates or find work elsewhere. Thus, there is always a push–pull relationship between mainstream comic publishers and the creative talent working for them. Creators in the comics industry are encouraged to bring their own ideas to the table, as Moore did, but the ability to use the intellectual property is doled out solely by the corporate copyright holder. Once the creation process is over, mainstream publishers such as DC Comics have little use for a writer, artist, or colorist's attachment to their labor; in fact, creators are expected to immediately move to other projects even before the final issue reaches market shelves, and the same was true for Moore, Gibbons, and Higgins (Gibbons 236).

This drive to extend the marketability of *Watchmen* also led to the eventual public falling out between Moore and DC Comics. Before *Watchmen*, the publication of comics was truly ephemeral; as Gibbons remembers, "in 1987, once a comic book series had run its course, that was pretty much the end of it. There might be sporadic foreign editions or reprints in the back of other titles, but even series conceived as self-contained stories, such as DC's *Camelot 3000*, were thereafter unavailable except in the back-issue bins" (237). A work's shelf life was over almost the moment it hit shelves. However, in an attempt to extend *Watchmen*'s lifespan, DC Comics collected the limited series into a single, bound collection for continued publication,[8] a new trend that eventually came to be called the "graphic novel" (Goggin and Hassler-Forest 2), both denoting the maturity of the work and its status as a self-contained story.[9]

However, while the graphic novel format did wonders for DC's bottom line, it also exploited a theretofore unforeseen loophole in comics publishing contracts. As was practice then and now, the copyright for mainstream comics initially belongs to the publisher, not the talent who worked to create it. DC's original contract with Moore and Gibbons stated that a year after *Watchmen* finished publication, the rights to the work would revert to them. But with the recreation of *Watchmen* into a graphic novel, the timeline for this transferal was reset, and continues to be reset with each subsequent reprint. When they began work on *Watchmen*, Moore and Gibbons reasonably expected that the rights to their creation would become theirs in 1989; instead, *Watchmen* has been in continuous print for more than thirty years. *Watchmen* can be found in bookstores—a far cry from the specialty comics shops more common in the 1980s—and has been listed as one of the greatest novels of the twentieth century by mainstream publications like *Time* magazine (Grossman); it is arguably the closest thing American comics has to a canonical text. This level of continued demand must be something beyond the wildest dreams of DC Comics, and they will never ever allow this fountain of revenue to slip through their fingers.

This newfound separation between *Watchmen* and its creators also drove wedges between the individual members of the creative team. Based on official and remembered histories of *Watchmen*, during production Moore, Gibbons, and Higgins worked as a collaborative and united front, but as soon as production had finished, this relationship of communal authorship began to fall apart. Once DC Comics made it clear that *Watchmen* ultimately belonged to them, the response to this turn of fortune varied wildly among the *Watchmen* creative team.

The reasons for this difference may be due to a number of factors. For Higgins, I believe that his response—that is, little to none—to the separation from the fruits of his labor has been mostly influenced by his initial role in the artistic hierarchy. Although the use of color is perhaps the most striking visual feature of comic books, the contribution of colorists has always been undervalued in the medium, making them the "*low man on the totem pole*" (Gibbons 164, emphasis original) in most comic production teams, if there is not a letterer, as was the case in *Watchmen*. As such, Higgins's contribution to *Watchmen* was unrewarded; he did not even receive royalties for *Watchmen* until publication of the 2005 digital edition (Gibbons 266). While this denial of royalties can be seen as unfair given his collaborative role in *Watchmen*'s production, this also meant that Higgins was largely unaffected by *Watchmen*'s afterlife as a graphic novel. He did not have anything to gain from the transferring of rights from DC to Moore and Gibbons or their retention by DC; there was no reason to maintain any concept of ownership over what he had helped create.

This attitude, however, seems to have changed with the introduction of the digital edition, which only became possible due to the continual consumer demand for *Watchmen* in its graphic novel form. After 2005, Higgins has become slightly more involved in the postproduction afterlife of *Watchmen*: he penned a short discussion of the coloring process in Gibbons's *Watching the Watchmen* (Gibbons 166–71) and was interviewed for a DVD extra for Zack Snyder's 2009 movie adaption. Additionally, Higgins granted legitimacy to the 2012 range of *Watchmen* prequel miniseries by contributing artwork for *The Curse of the Crimson Corsair*, a story in the same fictional series as "Marooned" that appeared in one- to two-page installments in the back of each of the other *Before Watchmen* issues, the publication of which both Gibbons and Moore rigorously disapproved. Although he is not as publicly connected to *Watchmen* as his collaborators, Higgins has become more amenable to asserting his creative contribution to the work as his efforts have been met with continued monetary reward.

The attitudes of Moore and Gibbons toward DC Comics' continued ownership of *Watchmen*, however, seem to have less to do with money than with feelings of creative control. Although *Watchmen* was never originally intended to be Higgins's future property, the original contract agreement did generate the expectation that it would one day belong to Moore and Gibbons; in short, the assumption of eventual ownership was both stated and implied. In addition, these two men worked closely together to craft *Watchmen* from its early preproduction stages, perhaps creating a greater sense of personal value invested in the limited series. For these reasons, both Moore and Gibbons have, in their own separate ways, asserted their ownership over *Watchmen* despite its legal status as a DC Comics property.

Gibbons, for his part, has forged an uneasy alliance with DC in the company's continued ownership of *Watchmen*. He has played a major role in promoting DC's continued publication of materials related to the original *Watchmen*, including the annotated edition and "making-of" book with his reminiscences referenced elsewhere in this chapter, by either endorsing or heavily contributing to these projects; similarly, Gibbons stated his approval for Snyder's film version in several interviews after watching a rough cut of the film (Leader). This contribution to DC's continued use of *Watchmen* has been predicated on his (at least partial) involvement in any *Watchmen*-related projects. In his 2009 art book/memoir *Watching the Watchmen*, Gibbons showed distinct territorial tendencies regarding *Watchmen* artwork. He was proud that, up to that point, he had drawn almost all artwork for *Watchmen* and its related merchandise; the only exclusion was an overnight poster project assigned to Kyle Baker by DC, as they could not get in touch with Gibbons quickly enough, an "impudence" which Gibbons "absolved" (Gibbons 261).

While Gibbons's feeling of both territorial ownership of *Watchmen* and support for several of DC's attempts to extend their control of it can seem paradoxical at first, a consideration of Moore and Gibbons's collaborative relationship could illuminate why those two instincts are not entirely contradictory. Although I have discussed at length Gibbons's contributions to Moore's writing of *Watchmen*, as well as his functional role as editor, in regard to prestige Moore and Gibbons were not considered equal as creative contributors. In traditional comics production procedure, the artist is often seen as an extension of the writer; the writer is the idea-generator, while the artist merely takes the writer's ideas and turns them into images and panels. This notion continues even in cases in which the artist takes on writer-like functions in the production of a comic. Despite the efforts of the other creative contributors, comics are still primarily associated with their writer in many people's minds; when reference is made to *Watchmen*'s creator, it is more likely to be referred to as "Alan Moore's *Watchmen*" than "Alan Moore and Dave Gibbons's *Watchmen*," much less "Alan Moore, Dave Gibbons, and John Higgins's *Watchmen*." This prioritizing of the writer as the main contributor is even consolidated by MLA citation rules, which compel scholars to cite *Watchmen* as the creation of "Moore et al." in lieu of listing all three names. Although the creative efforts of writer and artist are dependent on one another, the position of the writer continues to be privileged above all other roles.

Such expectations of the roles, respectively, of writer and artist, therefore, produce an imbalance between these two types of collaborators. As Wayne Koestenbaum notes in his exploration of Victorian male coauthors, there is almost always one partner who is considered less senior or less powerful position within a collaboration and thus "see[k] out a partner to attain power and completion" (Koestenbaum 2). As the artist, Gibbons's less powerful position within a partnership was both expected and maintained. During the creation of *Watchmen*, Gibbons seems to have attached his constrained authority over the limited series precisely through creative cooperation with Moore. Once DC exerted corporate control over the graphic novel, Gibbons maintained authority over *Watchmen*—to a limited extent—by re-establishing himself as a subordinate partner to DC. Although his creative partner has changed, Gibbons's status as the junior collaborator has not.

However, this attitude of cooperation with DC's corporate control of *Watchmen* does not appear to be extended to the company's attempts to further develop the property, particularly when these expansions are made without his inclusion as a subordinate collaborative partner. In 2009, Gibbons was heartily thankful that DC had recently decided against creating a prequel series showing the characters at various points before *Watchmen*; e.g., the Comedian's experiences in the Vietnam War (Gibbons 261). When DC Comics reversed course and announced the publication of a range of limited prequel series collectively known as *Before Watchmen* in 2012—including a *Comedian* miniseries set partly in the Vietnam War—Gibbons publicly stated that he did not approve of the new additions and did not consider them part of the *Watchmen* universe (McMillan). Similarly, when asked to comment on the then-ongoing *Doomsday Clock* sequel miniseries, Gibbons has said that he was not involved with the project and does not intend to even read it. To his mind, these extensions of the *Watchmen* mythos are not parts of the world he helped to cocreate and are therefore not worth consideration in connection to his work; it seems that by his reckoning, any product DC produces without involving him as a subordinate collaborative partner is not *Watchmen* at all.

Alan Moore, on the other hand, is now almost as famous for his ire toward DC Comics regarding their continued control over *Watchmen* as he is for his role in the work's creation. While Paul Levitz, who was president of DC Comics from 2002 to 2009, has claimed that Moore was initially amenable to the new *Watchmen* normal (Itzkoff), Moore recalls his relationship with DC souring quickly. According to Moore, an unnamed "highly placed person at DC" (qtd. in Johnston) had suggested to him and Gibbons that DC would not hand over the *Watchmen* universe to other creators if they maintained a working relationship with the company. Unlike Gibbons, who was willing to accept and collaborate with DC's continued control over their cocreation, Moore objected to this suggestion. If their control over *Watchmen* was only predicated upon their cooperation, then the moment they stepped out of line their creation would be taken completely out of their hands. This, in Moore's view, was a threat, especially in light of Moore's continued insistence that, after *Watchmen*—among several other properties he had written for DC Comics—finished its initial run, the rights for the limited series should have reverted to him. Moore left DC Comics shortly afterwards. Following legal fights with DC regarding the transmedia rights to other works he created both explicitly for DC Comics and for independent publisher America's Best Comics, an imprint of Wildstorm Comics which was then purchased by DC Comics in 1998 (Itzkoff), Moore largely left the comics industry altogether, surfacing in interviews for popular culture magazines to condemn the film adaptation of his works (Itzkoff; Johnston; Manning; Moore; Polo).[10]

At first, Moore's decision to completely relinquish all possible control over *Watchmen* and his other DC works rather than work with DC as a cocontroller of these works seems strange and counterproductive. As social commentator Susana Polo notes, Moore's falling out with DC and subsequent interviews has broken observers into two main groups: "those who believe that Moore is a paranoid weirdo, and those who believe that Moore is a *justifiably* paranoid weirdo" (Polo, emphasis original). Moore himself said later in interviews that he walked out because he "really do[es]n't respond well to being threatened" (qtd. in Johnston); however, I believe that this is not just a matter of personality, but a combination of two other factors. First, there were social expectations. Although comics have until recently not received the critical attention of other forms of new media such as film—hence the drive to represent more serious works as graphic novels—within the world of comics, the writer is most likely to be seen as the person from whom all of the work's plot, themes, and creative storytelling originate. Unlike Gibbons, whose artistic role had placed him in a secondary position from the beginning, Moore's role as writer always slated him (rightfully or not) as the major creative force in all his comic projects. Thus, Moore would have been more likely to be predisposed to the notion that *Watchmen* was "his," rather than a shared effort. To agree to DC's continued control of *Watchmen* and to act as costeward of the property rather than its sole owner, then, could be viewed as a step down in prestige, which may have been a step too far for Moore.

A contributing factor for this decision, however, could also have been the underlying politics of accepting a continually collaborative role, one which would result in fewer benefits than the limited-time collaboration required for *Watchmen*'s creation. For better or for worse, traditional western notions have promoted, among other values, independence and control. For Moore, I believe the reasons he entered his creative collaborations were for purely practical purposes. First, and perhaps most obviously, he was writing for comic books, and Moore was unable to produce the requisite amount and level of artwork within a reasonable timeframe, a requirement for the second motivation of earning a living.[11] Both of these reasons might have allowed him to function with unequal partnerships with DC Comics, Gibbons, and Higgins during *Watchmen*'s creation, but after its publication, the reasons for maintaining such a collaboration would have ceased. There were more comics to create, and although royalties continued to flow, these would continue regardless of Moore's future cooperation with DC Comics. As Koestenbaum notes in his study, the notion of collaboration has long carried a stigma—of collusion, of compromise, of a femininity his Victorian authors projected upon their created text (Koestenbaum 3, 8)—none of which could be easily reconciled with traditional expectations surrounding creative independence. Once the collaboration had produced its intended product, (i.e., *Watchmen*), the practical benefits of creative collaboration ceased to exist, leaving only traces of this stigma behind. Moore may have on some level felt the need to reassert a traditional authorial masculinity through insisting upon creative independence, as suggested by his insistence on *Watchmen* as his creation that should rightfully belong to him, not to DC Comics or to the men who helped him produce the work. When faced with the options to maintain traditional notions of artistic control and independence or to maintain involvement with his cocreation, Moore chose to fight for the former rather than accept the latter.

However, this decision to fight DC Comics for total control of works he cocreated was doomed before the start. Even though Moore publicly condemned the use of *Watchmen* after its initial publication and could reasonably argue that at the time when Moore, Gibbons, and Higgins signed their contracts with DC Comics the idea of allowing continued publication as a graphic novel was neither conceived of nor implied, the original contract explicitly stated that DC Comics owned all rights to the series until one year after its publication ceased. This arrangement was standard for the comics industry, and had become the norm since then-impoverished cocreators Jerry Siegel and Joe Schuster sold their rights to Superman to DC Comics in 1938 for $130 (Gibbons 237; E. Gardner; Cieply). Although *Watchmen* helped propel comics into a new era of storytelling, Moore's legal battles with DC did not bring the rights of comic creators into a similarly new age, despite all his contributions to the industry. The ground upon which Moore's legal struggles took place had been set against him decades earlier, and at the time of this writing does not seem likely to shift. *Watchmen* seems fated to remain with DC Comics in perpetuity.

Conclusion

Moore's journey as a collaborative author of *Watchmen* is, in a sense, reflected in Rorschach's characterization and storyline. Both are men characterized by extreme politics—Moore an anarchist, Rorschach a daily reader of the far-right *The New Frontiersman* (Moore et al., *Watchmen* 3.2.9–3.3.6)—and who have gained a reputation for his brilliance and (possibly justifiable) paranoia (Moore et al., *Watchmen* 1.12.4–5, 7.9.2; Moore et al., *Watchmen: The Annotated Edition* 17). Rorschach, like Moore, begins the events of *Watchmen* through writing: Moore through his proposal and scripts, Rorschach through his journal entries. While easily legible for readers, Rorschach's journal is said to be written in "either an elaborate cypher or handwriting too cramped and eccentric to be legible" (Moore et al., *Watchmen* 6.Sup.1)—a densely packed script in the literal sense, while Moore's scripts were only figuratively so.[12] However, the initial idea that spurred both men into the action of *Watchmen* (Rorschach's "mask killer" theory and much of Moore's original story proposal) threaten to reach a calamitous end through the ambush of legal authorities— Rorschach via arrest for his crimes, and Moore by DC's refusal to allow usage of the recently purchased Charlton characters. It is not until Rorschach (re)forges a collaborative investigation with Nite Owl II—a character inspired by one created by Gibbons in his adolescence (Gibbons 36)—that his focus is redirected to more fruitful avenues, much as Moore's collaboration with Gibbons and Higgins set the limit series toward its current acclaim.

Given these similarities, it is perhaps not surprising that both character and creator have found themselves with thematically similar endings. In both of *Watchmen*'s conclusions—as a story and as a publishable product—these men were the only ones to refuse to cooperate with their respective colleagues, to perpetuate an injustice each finds intolerable (Moore et al., *Watchmen* 12.20.7–9). Both refuse to compromise their integrity—as an uncompromising administer of self-imposed justice or as an independent creator—"not even in the face of Armageddon" (Moore et al., *Watchmen* 12.20.8), despite the practical realities that force their former collaborators to do so. Despite these attempts to maintain independence and control of their self-appointed domains, their efforts become unsustainable in the face of a higher authority. Moore's attempts to divorce himself from DC Comics proved futile, as his creations for America's Best Comics nevertheless became another set of Moore's creations for DC to exploit; Rorschach is murdered by the all-powerful Dr. Manhattan before he can escape Ozymandias's complex in Antarctica (Moore et al., *Watchmen* 12.24.4), ending his career as a masked vigilante and editing this author-figure out of existence. In the end, the fates of both of their creations, *Watchmen* and Rorschach's publishable journal, are left in the hands of strangers with no further influence by their original writers (Moore et al., *Watchmen* 12.32.6).

Much like its plot, the journey of *Watchmen* as a work has been one of unexpected twists and turns that have confounded traditional expectations of mainstream superhero comics. From the decision to rescind Moore's proposal to use Charlton characters after the initial agreement, to the unusually low amount of editorial interference from DC Comics during the series' production, to DC's perpetual continuation of the company's control via extended reprinting as a graphic novel, *Watchmen* is an example of both the fruitful results of collaboration between creators and the unequal power structures present within the industry that drive these creators apart from each other and from the products of their own labor. Although *Watchmen* has been considered one of the most impactful stories in of mainstream superhero comics, consideration of its production reveals the complicated realities of collaborative authorship and convergence culture that power the medium.

Traditional Process	Watchmen Process
1. Editor and writer discuss ideas.	1. Plot approved with new characters by DC Comics.
2. Writer creates pitch.	
3. Editor approves pitch.	2. Alan Moore (writer) and Dave Gibbons (penciler, inker, letterer) discuss ideas for issue by telephone.
4. Writer writes script with action, dialogue, and possibly panel layout suggestions.	
5. Editor approves script, gives script to penciler.	3. Moore writes script, gives it to Gibbons.
6. Penciler draws panels using script.	4. Gibbons creates art via penciling, then inking.
7. Editor approves penciled drawings ("pencils"), gives pencils to inker.	5. Gibbons makes copies and sends copies to DC Comics via Datapost.
8. Inker goes over pencils with ink.	6. Moore creates script for supplemental material.
9. Editor gives inked drawings to letterer and colorist.	7. Gibbons creates supplemental material.
10. Colorist selects colors.	8. John Higgins (colorist) confers with Moore and Gibbons about color ideas, selects colors.
11. Letterer adds dialogue bubbles, narration boxes, etc.	
12. Editor approves colors and lettering.	9. Final product sent to press.
13. Final product sent to press.	

CHAPTER 2

MARVEL MADNESS
Stan Lee and the "Marvel Method"

Introduction

Despite its depictions of larger-than-life characters, the world of comics production is a relatively anonymous one. Although their creations now saturate our media environment in blockbuster movies, cartoon and live-action television shows, and series featured on the ever-increasing number of streaming services (Netflix, Max, Disney+, etc.), for the majority of comics producers, their names and faces are generally unrecognizable to the public. While these creators' names are sometimes referenced by transmedia adaptors as a so-called "Easter egg" for dedicated comics readers—for example, locating a scene in season 2, episode 17 of the CW Network's *Arrow* TV show, titled "Birds of Prey," at the intersection of "Gail Street and Simone," a reference to Gail Simone, an acclaimed writer of DC Comics' *Birds of Prey* series, (Behring)—the difficulty of recognizing comics creators instantly is also often capitalized upon, as seen in the appearance of Jim Starlin, creator of the Marvel supervillain Thanos, in the post-Snap support group depicted in *Avengers: Endgame* (Russo and Russo). The Mad Titan Thanos may be instantly recognizable to the public, but the person who conceived of him can sit in the wake of his creation's path of destruction with relatively little notice by the average moviegoer.

One major exception to this norm of anonymity is Stan Lee, a cofounder of the powerhouse Marvel Comics who has been credited as creator of an impressive array of the company's iconic characters (including Spider-Man, the Fantastic Four, the Hulk, and the X-Men). Within the world of comics, Lee is credited with the creation of characters with real, human problems[1]—a move "not only toward irreverence and more engaging characters, but also away from young readers toward adolescent and college-aged readers" (Lopes 65). But due to decades of being a prominent spokesman for the value of comics—especially those produced by Marvel—as entertainment media and a long-standing tradition of appearing in television and film adaptions of his creations,[2] Stan "The Man" Lee became a pop-culture celebrity recognizable on sight by general audiences. With his seemingly limitless sense of humor and iconic mustache-and-sunglasses look, Stan Lee has been transformed into a figure almost as larger-than-life as his creations, a real-life champion of comics.

But following Lee's death on November 12, 2018, and the resulting tsunami of media reports praising Lee's impact upon comics and popular culture, there has been a swelling of opposing views in the popular conversation. These voices criticize the treatment of Lee as the genius behind some of America's favorite superheroes. In contradiction to the popular image of Stan Lee as "the single greatest contributor to comic book culture and creativity in the history of the format" (Consequences of Sound), this counter-narrative—which has existed within the comics industry to some extent for decades (Abad-Santos)—asserts that Lee falsely claimed to be the sole originator of many of the creations associated with him. Citing the innovative and highly collaborative writing process Lee standardized at Marvel Comics, now commonly referred to within the comics industry as "the Marvel Method,"[3] these critics assert that "Lee, for a long time, took most of the credit and usually left very little to spare for the co-creators, partners, and artists he worked with along the way" (Abad-Santos). Such critics see Lee as at best a glory hog and at worst a quasi-plagiarist, submitting the collaborative work of others to the eyes of the public attached only to his name.

These two popular conceptions of Lee can seem contradictory: Stan Lee is the genius creator of some of the most popular characters in twentieth-century popular culture and a creative powerhouse, or Stan Lee has built this public reputation by stealing credit from his collaborators, the unsung artistic geniuses, for decades. This debate can be heated, with little to no possibility of reconciliation between opposing sides.

This controversy speaks to a larger problem of discussing collaboration within creative industries, particularly in a corporate environment such as what we see in the "Big Two" companies in mainstream superhero comics (Marvel Comics and DC Comics). Namely, it is the issue of ascertaining creative origin. Anyone who has participated in a group project in which their work was misattributed to someone else—even mistakenly instead of maliciously—likely has an intuitive understanding of why such accreditation is important. If, as this book seeks to argue, collaboration is a primary component of creating mainstream superhero comics, then how do we make sure that we are giving credit where credit is due?

This may seem like a simple question with a simple answer; after all, don't they list the people's names on the cover for a reason? However, an examination of Stan Lee, the Marvel Method that he popularized, the resulting controversy regarding authorship, and the extant archival evidence demonstrates that when discussing creative collaboration in comics, the lines that purportedly divide the various creative roles are blurrier than they may initially seem.

Flipping the Script: Making Comics with the "Marvel Method"

Although Stan Lee was something of a workaholic—a trait he links to his Depression-era upbringing in his memoir, *Amazing,*

Fantastic, Incredible: A Marvelous Memoir (Lee, David et al.)[4]—Lee was especially busy during the 1960s. Two decades earlier, in 1941, Lee became comics editor for Timely Comics (Sanderson 19), which was officially renamed Atlas Comics in 1951, then whose name gradually changed to Marvel Comics in the early 1960s (DeForest). As the most senior (and for some time only) remaining member of Timely Publications' comics division, Lee was placed in charge of the Timely Comics bullpen, a skeleton crew that produced a single comic page per day on average (Frakes et al.).

The company's popularity grew at least partly due to the creation of several now-iconic Marvel characters within the first half of the 1960s: the Fantastic Four in 1961; the Hulk, Ant-Man, Thor, and Spider-Man in 1962; Sgt Fury, Iron Man, Doctor Strange, the X-Men, and the Avengers in 1963; Daredevil in 1964; and the Silver Surfer in 1966 (Frakes et al.). But increased popularity caused a greater strain to meet the increasing demand. Each of these properties required the continued production of comics in order to maintain their popularity, and while Marvel sales were increasing, its staff did not grow at a proportionate rate. Such limited growth from its late-1950s downsizing in the face of growing demand resulted in a staffing shortage, particularly in writers to create stories for Marvel's artists to depict in their comics (Raphael and Spurgeon 91).[5] Lee—in addition to his duties as Marvel editor, which included editing the "fan letters" page inside individual issues (a segment Lee put into practice at Marvel and which typically featured a monthly "Stan's Soapbox" column [Lee, David et al.])[6] and generating promotional copy for Marvel—also acted as writer for a number of comic books during this time. These added responsibilities also made further demands on Lee's limited time.

As discussed in the previous chapter, the production of the physical comic begins with the production of a script. Traditional comic book scripts contain plot, dialogue, and possibly a description of how the writer imagines the panel layout for the penciler (Bendis 28) and can thus take up several pages. Writing with this level of detail takes time, which Lee has admitted he simply did not have (Raphael and Spurgeon 91). In the face of this strenuous workload and limited staff, Marvel began to implement what was then a little-used method of writing comics, since dubbed "the Marvel Method," in order to meet deadlines (see table 2). Adopted to compensate for the overworking of the company's writers, the Marvel Method seeks to maximize production levels by reducing the effort and time the nominal writer spent per issue, particularly by increasing the creative workload of the visual artists on the team.

Like the traditional "full script" method, the Marvel Method starts with an idea. According to the prescribed process, the person acting as writer comes up with a series of major plot points that will be covered in an issue, which are approved by the editor. However, at this point the two processes drastically diverge. In the "full script" method of production, a longer, more exact outline is created for the penciler to work from when creating the comic panels. While these scripts are often not as detailed as Alan Moore's, full scripts typically describe at least general page-by-page actions and dialogue. However, in the Marvel Method a "full script" does not exist. There is no intermediary document between the pitch/synopsis and the first penciled pages. Instead, at first a basic story premise is pitched; when it is accepted, the synopsis is given to the penciler, who use this basic template and "goes off and *designs* the story" (Lee, David et al., emphasis original).

(During the early years of Marvel, barring the creation of a new series, which would require the allocation of new printing resources, Stan Lee acting as the publisher approved the proposals of Stan Lee acting as the idea man. One could imagine this "meeting" had few rejections or requests for changes, further expediting the process.)

This does not mean that writers using the Marvel Method no longer contribute creatively to the comic; on the contrary, the writer's public-facing work has only begun. At this point, the person acting as writer in the Marvel Method process receives a copy of the artwork, while the inker works on top of the original penciled panels, either simultaneously or shortly afterwards; in most explanations of the Marvel Method in how-to guides, the artwork that the person acting as writer receives is normally only done in pencils; these sheets, in their original and unscanned forms, are often called "pencils" within the industry. The writer then uses the illustrations to create suitable dialogue and narration, thereby creating the script in the end stages of the process, before coloring and lettering.

The Myth of the Solitary Comic Book Author

From this basic description of the Marvel Method's prescribed progress, it should be clear that the task of assigning the role of "writer" to a single person is more complicated than it appears at first glance. While one person is assigned to write—to place one word in front of another one—under the Marvel Method as it is normally represented, not all decisions we associate with writing are made by that person.

The summary of the Marvel Method that is provided in most general-audience introductions to the mainstream comic book industry calls individual collaborators "writer," "penciler," "inker," "letterer," and so on. Perhaps this is for expedience and to ensure the general audience understands, but such simplicity overlooks a necessary reality of the Marvel Method: an overview, by its nature, cannot encapsulate every detail of the story it summarizes.

The translation from what is on average a page-and-a-half summary to a full-length comic book requires a lot of fleshing out. The synopsis functions like a proposal: it provides a brief overview of an idea to be expanded upon later, once the basic concept has been approved.[7] After the handoff of the synopsis, at the penciler's desk, the majority of the comic book is created—not just its illustrations, but also the minor details that make up the issue. The synopsis is only two pages long; although the length of comics has varied over the industry's history, the final product usually stretches at least ten times as long to be considered a stand-alone story.[8]

This leaves the penciler, who is working with only the synopsis, to create the initial artwork by adding details as they see fit. That requires a great deal of creative expansion on the part of the penciler. While Lee was usually in the same building as the penciler during this era, he was working on multiple titles at once in addition to his duties as publisher. For anything not included in the synopsis, it was up to the penciler to fill in the gaps.

It is at this point in the process that we would find the invention of the story of the comic's issue, as we would normally think of it—that is, the panel-to-panel actions that take place. While the nominal writer begins the Marvel Method process by creating a synopsis as a foundational document, it is the penciler who takes the brief and often vague guidance given in the Marvel Method synopsis and makes the first permanent decisions regarding characterization, plot, and pacing; i.e., the choices that transform a string of words into a story. While "writer" may have been a job title at Marvel, it is the artist's pencil, not the writer's pen, that makes the first major passes that remain on the page in the role of the author under the Marvel Method.

Who Created What?: The Controversy

This part of the Marvel Method is the crucial point from which all other arguments regarding Stan Lee's purported creative genius and alleged credit-stealing derive. While it is no question that the comics that were created while Stan Lee was at least the nominal writer forever changed comics both as an industry and as a medium, the sometimes-heated debate regarding Lee and his contributions centers around how much of this legacy is actually warranted. The questions regarding collaborative authorship during this era at Marvel Comics are as fundamental as they are difficult: While the time period when Lee acted as writer and editor at Marvel certainly changed modern comics, how do we speak of his and his collaborators' creative contributions? How much of these comics came from Lee's mind alone? How many of the ideas for plot twists, character moments, and storylines that we currently consider to be Lee's should we instead rightfully attribute to someone else? And, perhaps most relevant to the subject of this book, is there any way we can know with certainty?

Confounding Contexts

When we approach this quandary, we should do so with an understanding of the environment in which Lee and his collaborators worked. These creators did not collaborate in a vacuum and were affected by their social environment, including the attribution practices that were already set in place in the comics industry as well as how the work they created affected both their own work and its reception by the media.

Golden Age (Non)Attribution

Discerning contributors to a particular issue of a comic might appear deceptively simple to a new comic book reader, especially today. The names all seem to be present on the cover, usually with a note that defines the role each person held on the creative team. As this project has demonstrated so far, however, this seemingly clear labeling is anything but precise, with so-titled writers and artists often sharing responsibilities behind the scenes regardless of whether they are using the traditional or the Marvel Method process. But this trend of improper attribution in the latter half of the twenty-first century is relatively transparent in comparison to early "Golden Age" (approximately 1938–56) publication practices of American superhero comics, which often only credited the title character's original creator(s) on the cover—if even that attribution was given fairly. For example, during this time the covers of DC Comics' tentpole *Batman* comic book series only named Bob

Kane—then (unfairly) treated as the sole creator of the caped crusader[9]—even after Kane stepped away from the comic book to focus on the Batman newspaper strips, forcing the actual contributors, including Jack Bunley, Dick Sprang, Fred Ray, Charles Paris, Alvin Schwartz, and Don Cameron, to effectively become ghostwriters and ghostartists (Daniels, *Batman: The Life and Times of the Dark Knight: The Complete History* 55).[10] In 1939, when Stan Lee first entered the world of comics as a Timely Comics assistant, the industry was in the dark ages of acknowledged coauthorship, placing emphasis on an intellectual property's originator, not the creators caretaking it.

According to comics historian Jim McLauchlin, it was Lee who implemented changes, many of which now industry standards, which more fairly gave credit to a comic's contributors. The shift from anonymous creators ghostwriting and ghostdrawing for a potentially long-gone inventor to the current style of explicit (though flawed) attribution came about in large part as a result of Lee's efforts to market Marvel Comics.

First, he had the current creators on a particular project listed on the cover along with their official roles (Frakes et al.), a practice that had fallen by the wayside during the 1940s (Gabilliet 67). While it is true that these accreditations separated the cocreators into rigid roles that might not have reflected the full extent of their actual contributions, this was nonetheless a major step towards proper accreditation of artistic labor. Although DC Comics restarted the practice before Marvel (Gabilliet 67), Marvel Comics took it a step further by "building personality around these people," giving them catchy, typically alliterative personality-themed nicknames (e.g., Jazzy John Romita Sr., Gentleman Gene Coleman, and Jolly Jack Kirby [Frakes et al.]), to incorporate them as part of the brand's image of a publication that was as filled to the brim with colorful characters as the comics they produced. This marketing of the writers and artists as Marvel personalities went so far as to transform the creators into consumable characters in 1964, when one of the many incentives for becoming a member of the Merry Marvel

Marching Society (the first of a long string of Marvel-sponsored fan clubs) was a 33⅓ rpm record introducing "The Voices of Marvel" (Lee, David et al.).[11] Not only did Lee's decision bring the creators at Marvel Comics out of obscurity and into the spotlight, but it also made his cocreators and his interactions with them an inextricable part of Marvel's self-branding.

This image of Marvel as "a bastion of collegiality and capering fraternal humor, a 'bullpen' of close, like-minded eccentrics who turned Marvel's editorial offices into a friendly, comfortable, free-wheeling shambles" (Hatfield 78) was critical to Marvel's branding while Stan Lee acted as editor-in-chief, and still influences how fans think about the company in this era and beyond (Stein 137). While this move to commodify the creative workers at Marvel as a means of bolstering the company's profits is worthy of its own criticism—after all, it literally turns these living, breathing creative individuals into products to be sold by Marvel—it does represent an increased acknowledgment of the collaborative contributions of these creators.

Rippling Outward: Impact of Artists' Marvel Method Contributions

But just because Marvel Comics began to acknowledge the creators who were actively working on a comic, rather than just initial creators, and incorporated their public images as part of the company's branding does not mean that this attribution was entirely accurate.

In the previous chapter discussing the collaboration that created *Watchmen*, we saw that the planning conversations between Alan Moore and Dave Gibbons had a major impact on the final product. Although the collaboration between Moore, Gibbons, and Higgins followed the more traditional comics creation process, small details suggested by Gibbons—the addition of a smiley pin on the Comedian's design, the possible lack of interest in superhero comics in a reality of real-life "heroes," and so on—had the potential to have a monumental impact on the final miniseries as we know it today. But the level of impact created by the inclusion of Gibbons's suggestions is limited by the very nature of the work as a limited series intended to stand separately from the rest of DC Comics' standard storytelling universes.[12] Even though later DC publications have tried (and thus far, largely failed) to permanently intertwine the "main" DC universe with that of *Watchmen*, the lasting effects of Moore, Gibbons, and Higgins's initial work on other titles published by DC Comics and the larger superhero has been largely tonal and/or philosophical.

However, the structural boundaries delineating the extent of such contributions did not typically exist when one of Lee's artistic collaborators carried out the expansion of a Marvel Method summary to full plot. Although the penciler had a rough guide of the story via the synopsis and a rough estimate of how long the penciled story needed to be, that left room for the penciler's own ideas within the panels, and how much liberty these pencilers were able (or perhaps were willing) to take could vary. Penciled versions that returned to Lee could follow what he outlined, with the addition of small events or subplots to extend the skeletal plot of the synopsis. However, the outlined story also could have undergone radical transformations while it was on the penciler's desk.

Lee's longtime cocreator, artist Jack Kirby, was particularly well-known for making massive changes from synopsis to pencils. As John Romita Sr., another collaborator with Lee, recounted, "I used to hear [Lee and Kirby] plotting stories, but I don't remember them ever agreeing on anything. Jack had his own idea. He went home and did his version. And Stan, when he got the pages, said 'Gee, Jack didn't remember anything we talked about'" (Frakes et al.). While these variations could be minimally consequential, others could have a powerful impact on the Marvel universe. In one famous instance, when Lee received the pencils for *Fantastic Four* #48 (published March 1966), which was meant to introduce readers to the planet-consuming cosmic entity known as Galactus, he was met with an unexpected sight: flying around Galactus was a man on what seemed to be a flying surfboard, a figure that Lee had decidedly not mentioned in his synopsis. Upon questioning, Kirby said that he figured that, as a dread cosmic planet-eater, Galactus would likely have a herald: "someone to fly around and find planets for him to gobble up" (S. Lee, *The Ultimate Silver Surfer*). After brief consideration, Lee reportedly decided this was a smart addition. But the flying surfboard? Because, said Kirby, surfing was a popular trend among young people at the time. Besides, "I'm tired of drawing spaceships!" (S. Lee, *The Ultimate Silver Surfer*). Since the character lacked a name, Lee—a fan of alliterative superhero titles and a "burning desire for visual imagery" (S. Lee, *Part Five: The Fiend Flies by Night!* 26)—named Kirby's creation the Silver Surfer, a character widely popular with college students in the following decade.

This popularity of the Silver Surfer adds an extra layer of complication upon discussion of artists' Marvel Method contributions. While the popularity of *Watchmen* as well as its adaptations and spinoffs are at least as great as that of several Marvel properties, the presence of these changes within the so-called "Marvel Universe," rather than in an alternate part of the company's fictional multiverse, meant that artists' contributions could spread beyond the confines of the issue or series that the creator worked on. Characters such as the Silver Surfer could appear in future stories, or even as a visiting character in other titles, and plot points introduced by the penciler potentially could lay the groundwork for future story arcs in the same or a different series.[13] Because of the radical changes the penciler could make to the story in the transition from the synopsis to full comic, and then from published comic to its impact on the wider product line, discussions of assigning credit for any particular comic created via the Marvel Method can been particularly fraught.

The effects of penciler's decisions during this phase of the Marvel Method, such as Kirby's choice to create the Silver Surfer, could thus ripple outwards to influence the course of Marvel Comics for decades. Beginning in the late 1950s, the student press became the third medium (after newspapers and comic magazines) to welcome comics (Gabilliet 63), and Marvel Comics' pivot toward more young adult–centric material coincided with this rise college-aged young people paying serious attention to this medium. As the University of California's humor magazine, *The California Pelican*, once quipped, Marvel Comics was "the greatest revolution in literature on campus since the foldout nude" (Frakes et al.). The popularity of the Silver Surfer, along with that of the supernaturally gifted Dr. Strange, prompted dozens of student groups to invite Lee, as the face of Marvel Comics, to speak at college campuses across the United States in the 1970s (Frakes et al.). These visits, in which Lee was acting as both representative of Marvel's publisher and as (co) creator of numerous popular characters, generated a wellspring of inspiration by acting as a site of exchange between converging media cultures. After speaking about comics—typically arguing for the value of comics as an underrespected storytelling medium, a favorite talking point of his—for approximately twenty minutes, Lee would take questions from the audience. The fans, faced with a once-in-a-lifetime opportunity to pose questions to a popular creator, would ask Lee about Marvel-related topics to gain inside knowledge, something particularly valued in many avid fan cultures (Jenkins, *Convergence Culture* 27). Lee, in turn, used these question-and-answer sessions to gauge what interested college-aged readers, a major segment of Marvel's intended audience, and Marvel Comics adopted these ideas to make the company's more appealing, creating a synergy between consumers and Lee, who was acting as both corporation figurehead and creator. Although the original synopsis did not call for the creation of the Silver Surfer, Kirby's independent streak as penciler inadvertently seeded avenues through which Marvel Comics as a company could continue its development as a powerhouse in popular young adult culture.

Stan the Media Man

This very popularity placed Marvel Comics—and especially Lee—in the spotlight. As enthusiasm for comics—and especially Marvel

Comics—began to spread out of its traditionally niche, child-oriented market, news publications began to turn their eye toward the companies that created these new media sensations. As the company's figurehead, Lee was featured in numerous extra-Marvel publications regarding the company and comics in general during the late 1960s and 1970s. In these articles and interviews, we can see both how Lee himself spoke about his cocreators and how journalists from that time viewed these partnerships.

While Lee does exude a certain public persona in these appearances—the kind of hip male-coded braggadocio that could lead Lee, a man in his forties, to nickname himself "Stan 'The Man' Lee"[14]—he does seem to share credit in his interviews, promoting his cocreators as part of the Marvel team. But instead of taking cues from Lee's public acknowledgments of Marvel comics as the products of multiple authorship, early comics journalists seem insistent on portraying Lee as the solitary genius that revolutionized comic books.

In one often-cited instance, the *New York Herald Tribune*'s Nat Freeland approached Lee in 1965 proposing an interview regarding the rise and current state of Marvel Comics. Despite being offered a solo interview, which would have been a perfect opportunity for Lee to publicly claim sole credit for the company's success, he insisted that Freeland also include Jack Kirby since they were acting as cocreators for many of the properties that Freeland wanted to focus on (Frakes et al.). In Freeland's writeup of the interview, Lee is clear that his collaborators—for example, Ditko and Kirby—are major contributors to Marvel's success. In the article, Lee reiterates that he writes the dialogue to a comic after the artist draws the panels and according to their marginal comments—reflecting his other public explanations of the Marvel Method, including the one in the first-anniversary issue of *Spider-Man* (Lee, Ditko et al.)—even going so far as to admit to Freedland that "I don't plot Spider-Man any more. Steve Ditko, the artist, has been doing the stories" (Freedland).

At every step of the interview, Lee took pains to emphasize the contributions of others, even at the expense of his own. However,

Freeland evidently did not share Lee's vision of Marvel Comics as a collaborative enterprise. When it was published in the Sunday edition on January 9, 1966, Freedland treated the artistry of Marvel Comics as exclusively Lee's. For the first four of the article's five and a half columns, Freedland almost breathlessly recounts Lee's popularity and how he "dreamed up 'The Marvel Age of Comics'" (Freedland). When the article shifts, begrudgingly, to discuss Lee's collaborator, Freedland's view of Kirby, as a person and as an artist, is demeaning:

> Here [Lee] is in action at his weekly Friday morning summit meeting with Jack "King" Kirby, a veteran comic book artist, a man who created many of the visions of your childhood and mine. The King is a middle-aged man with baggy eyes and a baggy Robert Hall-ish suit. He is sucking a huge green cigar and if you stood next to him on the subway you would peg him for the assistant foreman in a girdle factory. . . .
> He has kind of a high-pitched voice. (Freedland)

Although in their interview Lee explicitly positioned the artists at Marvel as creative equals, if not more important than himself, and as partners in the creation of their comics, Freeland insisted not on acknowledging their contributions but on framing Lee as the fountain from which all of Marvel's hipness and originality flowed.

Early comics journalists, it seems, were so enraptured by the idea of singular authorship, what Stillinger calls the "myth of solitary genius," that they denied the reality of coauthorship, even when it was staring them in the face in the form of Lee's public admissions. In their urgency to establish comic books as a legitimate form of literature, to counteract a sense of inferiority also felt by Lee during his career (see S. Lee, *Are You Old Enough to Read Comicbooks?*), these enthusiastic journalists denied the collaborative nature of creating superhero comics to align the narrative about comics with the then-predominant thinking regarding artistic genius as a solitary activity.

While this strategy may have contributed to our current under-standing of comics as a legitimate storytelling medium, it had last-ingly detrimental effects on all members of the Marvel creative teams. This lack of attribution by journalists has been viewed by several comic historians, as well as Steve Ditko himself, as a compelling factor behind both Ditko and Kirby's leaving Marvel (Ditko; Abad-Santos; Riesman). Although Ditko and Kirby continued creating their own solo projects afterwards, the adamant adherence to the myth of the solitary genius drove apart what could arguably be one of the most productive partnerships in the history of mainstream comics.

Additionally, these journalists' denial of coauthorship in the name of the medium's acceptance warped how Lee, the man to whom they attached all their notions of sole creatorship, was perceived after comics' artistic legitimacy was established. When these pieces were published, establishing comics as a serious subject of discus-sion, an art form produced by geniuses, became the sole mission; sharing artistic credit with Lee's collaborators would only muddy the waters. While not exactly exemplifying the heights of journalis-tic integrity, such a rhetorical strategy seems reasonable given their cultural context. However, decades later, when Marvel creations are featured in blockbuster movies during every major movie season, it is no longer necessary to establish comics as an artistic medium. With no such status of inferiority as a medium, without a driving need to convince the general public that comic books are a valid form of entertainment, these ascriptions of all creative credit to Lee unfairly assigns him credit for the labor of others despite his own efforts to the contrary. Despite his own public statements, in publica-tions both by Marvel Comics and by contemporary journalism, that he was, at most, the manager of the Marvel idea factory, he became the victim of his contemporary public's refusal to acknowledge their beloved comic books as group projects and the entrenched, single-minded portrayal of Lee as a solitary genius. It is a terrible further irony that, because of their insistence on ignoring Lee's testimony of the Marvel Method's collaborative process, journalists inscribed him in the public consciousness as a character who stole the ideas of others to claim them as his own: turning Lee into a real-life comic book villain of their making.

All three of these contexts combine to create an environment that makes delineating each contributor's input to the final product exceedingly difficult. Given that Golden Age attribution practices often did not acknowledge creative workers at all if they were not a property's (official) originators, a media environment that seemed to be dedicated to the valorization of a single contributor is not surprising. However, the ways in which artists' ideas could trigger a domino effect and change the face of Marvel Comics, as did Kirby's idea for the Silver Surfer, demonstrates that the contributions of these unacknowledged cocreators can and did have a major impact on the company, characters, and stories that are popularly associated with Stan Lee.

But can we possibly determine which ideas, if any, are an individual's contributions? Unfortunately, looking at the final product does not bear much fruit, and delving into the physical evidence that we do have of these stories' creation through the Marvel Method does not make the attempt to determine individuals' contributions much easier.

The "Marvel Method" as Seen in the Stan Lee Papers

Through the passage back-and-forth between desks and mediums, creative origins can become impossible to see in an examination of only the final product. When it comes to multiple sources of creativity coming together, it can be enticing to think that there should be an easy source through which we can decipher what idea came from where and at what point of the process. If there were such a source, it would be in the draft materials that were created in the various stages of the Marvel Method. If we were able to examine these draft documents, it bears to reason, we would be able to better understand not only the Marvel Method process as a whole, but also how individual contributions helped to shape the initial ideas into their final, published form.

This idea is not new in certain areas of academic research. For example, in the study of James Joyce, the twentieth-century Irish author whose works have both delighted and confounded modern readers, we have an extensive collection of biographies, Joyce's handwritten notebooks, multiple drafts, and even annotated corrections to initial print proofs that can be used to track down Joyce's notetaking and scribbling from various sources for possible inclusion in expansive works such as *Ulysses* and *Finnegans Wake*. As long as someone can decipher Joyce's handwriting (often cramped and hurried even before Joyce's "feeble eyesight" [Birmingham 10] deteriorated) or have access to either print or digital recreations of these materials, any dedicated scholar or otherwise curious mind could theoretically find the source of many of Joyce's countless references and inspirations. This was just for one man leaving physical evidence of his own, solitary work. Surely, someone with experience with such types of scholarship may ask, a process requiring multiple drafting stages being passed back and forth between individuals would leave behind a similarly thorough amount of evidence?

In this case, the most publicly availably resource to turn to is the archival evidence found within the Stan Lee archive at the University of Wyoming's American Heritage Center. In this archive, Lee's personally donated collection of papers, which is contained within 196 boxes and includes times dating from 1926 to 2011, currently serves as the largest collection of Lee's papers, drafts, correspondence, and other memorabilia.[15] Thus, it is the best resource for finding and analyzing physical evidence of how Lee and his cocreators collaborated via the Marvel Method.

However, the size of an archive does not guarantee that it contains the materials you are looking for. During my time in the Stan Lee Papers, I specifically searched for any items that were connected to the creative process. In my search, I found materials for all production phases for only two Marvel Comics issues: *Solarman* #2: "This Silent Death, This Hostage Earth" (S. Lee, *Solarman* #2: *"This Silent Death, This Hostage Earth" Synopsis*; S. Lee, *Solarman* #2: *"This Silent Death, This Hostage Earth" Script*; Zeck), the second part of a two-issue *Solarman* limited series; and the one-shot megacomic *Spider-Man Kingpin: To the Death!* (DeFalco; S. Lee, *Spider-Man (Kingpin) Special: "To the Death"*; Romita Sr.; Romita Sr. and Lee; Lee, Romita Sr. et al.).

But neither of these sets of materials seem suitable as materials to be analyzed analysis of the "real" Marvel Method, for different reasons. For the set of materials for *Solarman* #2, the character is not a property that Marvel Comics owns (Gibbs et al.).[16] Instead, Marvel's publication of *Solarman* was only the 1989 limited series and an unsold animated TV show pilot (Gibbs et al).[17] Because this was a temporarily licensed property, and I could not find the details of this licensing agreement in the archive or elsewhere, I am unable to delineate which discrepancies from the idealized Marvel Method that is shared in public-facing industry guides are due to inter-company arrangements and which result from how the Marvel Method may have varied between prescribed theory and actual practice. For the materials relating to *Spider-Man Kingpin: To The Death!*, it is the synopsis itself that causes me to set it aside from this study. Although this set of draft materials mostly follows the Marvel Method's creation process, the synopsis created by Tom DeFalco is written with page-by-page action summaries, akin to what would be expected if they were following the traditional "script" method. Therefore, this set, though completed, may not be indicative of the Marvel Method for the purposes of our study.

Then there is the matter of sample size. While it may simplify things to focus solely on these only two complete sets—through which we can see each step of the process—to place attention on just two completed sets of documents would fail to acknowledge the wide variety found in the archive, likely skewing our understanding of how collaborative authorship worked when these creators worked together via the Marvel Method.

While cataloging the archive's complete contents is far beyond the scope of this project, the remainder of this chapter thus focuses on independent items from Marvel Method stages, even though few of the items mentioned have more than a single Marvel Method stage within the archive. I shall also examine what these items could mean concerning the individual contributions of Stan Lee and his collaborators within the Marvel Method process and the larger discussion regarding collaborative work.

The Synopsis

Despite the importance of the synopsis in beginning the creation of the comic, this initial write-up appears to have been given the least import as a draft version of the final product. Even given the brevity (and thus easy storage) of such a document, few early plot synopses remain in the archives in comparison to the other in-progress writings (pencils, scripts, and final products). During my forty hours in the Stan Lee archive, these synopses were the most difficult to find of all the Marvel Method phases.

It is possible that the relative lack of synopses within the Stan Lee Papers may be due to their treatment as ephemeral placeholders for the "real" scripts that were to come later in the process and that synopses were disposed once they had achieved their purpose of conveying the official writer's basic ideas to the penciler. Perhaps these synopses do not exist in the Lee archive, which Lee himself donated to the American Heritage Center in batches between 1981 and 2011 (Stan Lee Papers 1926–2011), because they were not kept long enough to be included.

Alternatively, the rarity of these synopses in the Lee archive may be because they might not have been paper documents. Although working together to create comics over a long distance was not impossible before the rise of the internet—as can be seen with the creation of *Watchmen* in the previous chapter—the logistics of such an undertaking added an incentive to bring all collaborators together to work in the same physical space. While examples of written synopses do exist, perhaps most idea-sharing at this early stage took place informally, with emphasis given to the expedience of a short walk to talk to someone versus the effort of writing one's ideas down.

Although never explicitly mentioned, this potential use of oral rather than written synopses is suggested by both contemporary and later portrayals of the Marvel Method. In the "How Stan Lee and Steve Ditko Create Spider-Man!" spotlight in 1963's *The Amazing Spider-Man Annual* #1, Lee is shown holding a paper—perhaps a written synopsis—while verbally telling artist Steve Ditko about his idea for a new issue at a "story conference" (Lee, Ditko et al. 39). Many years later, in Lee's 2015 graphic memoir, a younger Lee is shown animatedly orating a story idea into a cassette recorder at a home office (Lee, David et al.). John Romita Sr., then a junior artist at Marvel, recalls overhearing Stan Lee and Jack Kirby "plotting stories" in the Marvel offices (Frakes et al.). Similarly, Steve Ditko's 1990 account of the process emphasized that "Stan provided the plot ideas. There would be a discussion to clear up anything, consider options and so forth" (Raphael and Spurgeon 91).

These portrayals of the story synopsis as a process of verbal recounting may, of course, be portrayed inaccurately for various reasons. After all, the primary purpose of the section of *Amazing Spider-Man Annual* #1 was to entertain and inform readers of general practice, not inform future comics scholars about the exact nature of the Marvel Method; similarly, the scene depicting Lee at his home office functions primarily to lighten the memoir's tone after a discussion of the Lee family difficulties,[18] and any audio recordings Lee made could have later been transcribed as written synopses to be given to the pencilers. However, Romita Sr.'s reminiscences indicate that at least part of the early planning stages of the Marvel Method took place not on paper, where a scholar can easily trace an idea's origins, but orally, where it can leave little physical evidence.

No matter whether the truth is found through one of these explanations, a combination, or another reason entirely, evidence of all

Marvel Method stages for any given comic collected within Lee's papers at the American Heritage Center is rare. Despite that, it is possible to examine the existing written synposes to see the primordial shape of Lee's original ideas early in the Marvel Method process in relation to their final, published versions.

Because these synposes were general and brief, there is little room for specific details. Take, for example, the synopsis of *Fantastic Four* #1, written for a fall 1961 release, which is only a page and a half long. Comics writer Brian Michael Bendis says this falls well within the expected length range for a Marvel Method script in the industry today (S. Lee, *Synposes: The Fantastic Four July '61 Schedule (#1)*; Bendis 28).[19,20] However, the level of detail in and around this document—what's there, what's not—is as an illustrative demonstration of how ambiguous the synopsis stage of the Marvel Method could be.

The first ambiguous aspect of this document surrounds its location in the Stan Lee Papers. Every collection has its own organization system, which originates either from the original person or group who donated the collection to the holding archive (typically in a way that made sense to them) or from those who maintain the archive. The Stan Lee Papers at the American Heritage Center is housed in boxes and "were donated by Stan Lee at various times between 1981 and 2011" (Stan Lee Papers 1926–2011), and in most boxes these were divided into folders. However, the organization of the folders within boxes in the Stan Lee Papers is somewhat perplexing. This synopsis, with a 1961 date as its header, was found in Box 52, Folder 7; also in this box were scripts for a 1983 TV show (Folder 14) as well as 1978–81 daily comic strips for the Incredible Hulk newspaper comic (Folders 3–5). It is only the title of the document—*Synopses: The Fantastic Four July '61 Schedule (#1)*—that dates this synopsis.

However, we can still be reasonably sure that this document was not created after the fact for one simple reason: there are too many discrepancies between the story outlined in this initial document and the one that appears in the final publication of *Fantastic Four* #1. The general ideas that Lee lays out for Jack Kirby in this synopsis often found their way onto the final pages in some form; however, as we will explore shortly, there are several notable differences between the two versions of this story. If this synopsis had been created after the fact, then it would stand to reason that there would be a closer alignment between "first draft" and final product. Instead, reading this document in conjunction with the published issue shows how ideas for characters and plot could transform over the course of the Marvel Method process.

As the issue is meant to introduce the Fantastic Four as a team made of new characters (or, in the case of Johnny Storm, aka the Human Torch, a character reimagined with a great deal of creative license),[21] Lee appears to have kept a grasp on the characters' personalities and their accidental and confused approaches to their new abilities. *Fantastic Four* #1 shows the Human Torch's fire and flight inconveniently cut short while is he midair (Lee, Kirby, Klein et al. 8), reflecting Lee's idea that one of his weaknesses should be that his capabilities "[don't] last for more than 5 minutes [. . . and he] can't flame on at least 5 minutes after he's gotten back to normal" (S. Lee, *Synposes: The Fantastic Four July '61 Schedule* [#1]). Reed Richards (alias Mr. Fantastic), the young scientist leading the group, and Ben Grimm (also known as The Thing), the "husky, brutish" (S. Lee, *Synposes: The Fantastic Four July '61 Schedule* [#1]) pilot, struggle for the affections of Sue Storm, aka Invisible Girl,[22] during which the two men discover the extent of their abilities (Lee, Kirby, Klein et al. 12). Sue, for her part, is given little treatment as a character beyond her romantic relationship: "[s]he is Reed's girl friend [*sic*]. She's an actress. Beautiful, glamourous" (S. Lee, *Synposes: The Fantastic Four July '61 Schedule* [#1]). In this synopsis and the early issues of *Fantastic Four*, she does not contribute much in terms of story other than as an object for Richards and Grimm to fight over, and she looks beautiful for the male-coded audience, prompting the creation of an issue in which the male members of the team respond to (vaguely fictionalized) fan mail criticizing her as a purposeless character (Lee, Kirby, Ayers et al. 9–10). Additionally, the origin of the group's powers in their exposure to cosmic rays during their unauthorized space travel exists much in the same form as in Marvel comics today.

But even the details provided in this synopsis were often open to change and were stated vaguely, informally, and even inconsistently in the synoptic documents themselves, inviting the penciler's discretion. When discussing the invisibility powers of Sue Storm, for example, Lee suggests that her inability to turn her clothes similarly invisible may require changing the gimmick of her character (S. Lee, *Synposes: The Fantastic Four July '61 Schedule* [#1]), as he worries that her need to remove them in order to be fully invisible may be "to [*sic*] sexy" (S. Lee, *Synposes: The Fantastic Four July '61 Schedule* [#1]). As Lee was test-driving his idea of writing a comic catered to older readers "that have *more depth* and *substance* to them" (Lee, David et al., emphasis original) rather than catering to sex appeal, Lee seems to convey the fine line that he wanted the series to walk between mature and adult storytelling.[23] Likewise, while Ben Grimm retains a rough character in the final version, the group is no longer in danger of his sabotaging their efforts for the sake of gaining Sue's attention or for similar selfish purposes, as Lee had originally suggested in this synopsis (S. Lee, *Synposes: The Fantastic Four July '61 Schedule* [#1]).

Lee routinely suggests aspects of the teams' storyline with qualifying hedge-words like "might," "maybe," etc. The items in Lee's synopsis that at first seem firm in his mind later become changeable; while he begins by firmly stating that the titular characters receive their powers during an unauthorized space flight to Mars, Lee ends this summary with an aside, "maybe we better make this a flight to the STARS, instead of just to Mars, because by the time this mag goes on sale, the Russians may have already MADE a flight to Mars!" (S. Lee, *Synposes: The Fantastic Four July '61 Schedule* [#1], emphasis original), a change that appears in the final version. Even the length of sections, often described in detail in a full comics script, are mutable in this early document. At the beginning of the document, Lee breaks the introductory issue into two chapters: the first six pages long, the second five (S. Lee, *Synposes: The Fantastic Four July '61 Schedule* [#1]). Then, at the end of the synopsis, Lee originally typed that his vision for the next issue would also include two chapters "in which the Fantastic Four undertakes their first case" (S. Lee, *Synposes: The Fantastic Four July '61 Schedule* [#1]), both consisting of eight pages, but this new estimate has been crossed out in pen and amended in Lee's handwriting to suggest three chapters of three, five, and five pages apiece. But none of these chapter length predictions remained true by the time the comic reached the printers. In the final version of *Fantastic Four* #1, there are two chapters. The first, thirteen pages long, portrays the events initially described in the synopsis as a single chapter, not two. Even when the first chapter of the final issue is divided into its two main subsections—the introduction to the characters' abilities as they assemble at Reed Richard's signal and the relating of their origin story—these sections take up eight and five pages, not six and five as originally laid out by Lee. The second official chapter of the issue, the plot for which is only nine words long in the synopsis, consists of another eleven pages showing the team wrangling with the underground supervillain, The Moleman. Both the introductory plotline and the future issue instead appear as a singular issue, meaning that the entirety of the issue's second chapter came subsequent to this draft. Even though this synopsis was meant to be the guiding document for Kirby as a penciler, then, the differences between synopsis and final product show that nothing at this stage was set in stone.

Penciling

The seemingly cut-and-dried step of copying the artwork for the Marvel Method writer's later writing work appears to have been more complicated in practice than in theory, particularly in later projects in which Lee was involved. According to the prescribed process, copies of the initial panel drawings were made for the writer once the editor approved the pencils. While the creation of a scriptwriting copy before inking may have been a consistent practice in the early 1960s, when Lee was both writer and editor, for most of his projects adherence to this order seems to have relaxed over the decades as Lee spent less time in an active managerial role. In 1986, Lee received panel drawings for *The Mighty Thor* #385, "Be Thou God, or Monster!," which were already in the inking stage to create the final script (Lee, Shooter et al.). These partially inked pages were accompanied by a small note from either Ralph Macchio or Tom DeFalco (editor and chief editor for the issue, respectively) apologizing for the premature inking, blaming a communication issue, suggesting that scanning the panels at such a late stage might have been a managerial oversight and not an intentional speeding-up of an already expedited process (Lee, Shooter et al.).

This move towards simultaneous inking slowly evolved from accident into universal practice by 1998, when Marvel letterer John Workman wrote a letter to Lee complaining about the "near-universal acceptance" of the practice at Marvel Comics (Workman). In his response, which was stapled to Workman's letter in the Stan Lee Papers, Lee informs Workman that he no longer oversaw the day-to-day details at Marvel Comics (Workman).[24] Whether it is due to the increased reliance on computers and overlay publishing allowing for a less stringent adherence to the traditional Marvel Method process, as Workman suspects, or due the decreasing presence of those editors reliant on the process, the inking of the penciled pages and the scripts that accompanied them on the page became increasingly divorced from one another, becoming a branching process in which they eventually were joined together to create the final issue.

This increasing incidence of simultaneous inking could have lasting effects on the final product. According to anecdotal reports, such as the one above, Lee often had comments and suggestions regarding the penciler's artistic decisions, like encouraging artists to redraw panels to have more expressive compositions,[25] including asking Jim Shooter to make the innocent civilians appear more horrified at the sudden appearance of the Hulk, or drawing on top of his copy of the scanned penciled version in blue pen to combine two smaller panels into one and telling the penciler to "move [the drawing in the first of the panels] over" to the center of the new, combined panel (Lee, Buscema et al.). While the penciler's decisions to expand upon the story strictly as outlined in the synopsis or to include entirely new material seem to have remained largely untouched by Lee when he was acting as writer/editor, inking the pages before or while the final script was being written effectively prohibited the number of changes the writer could suggest for the visual art. As Workman says in an argument reminiscent of Walter Benjamin, the practice of inking before the finalization of script and lettering forces the visual artist "to have to settle for more generic and less specific looks on their faces" as opposed to tailoring expressions based on what they were saying, and "[t]his cause[s] a 'break' between the dialogue and the visual and weaken[s] the effectiveness of the work" (Workman; see Benjamin). Instead of acting as a cohesive whole and seamlessly blending verbal and visual information, forcing the finalization of a comic's illustration and narration to happen simultaneously, with little communication between both creators, might cause the medium's submodes to act in competition with one another, hampering the artistic potential of the final product.

The Script

Regardless of whether the panels had entered the inking stage, once the nominal writer was given the copied panel drawings, they set about writing a new document to accompany the pencils: the script, which included the dialogue and narration as they would appear in print. Using the synopsis as a basic guide, the writer's new script was tailored to match the drawings provided by the penciler. This flips traditional notions about the role of comic book writer and comic book artist. Instead of the artist (theoretically, according to industry tradition) acting as the enactor of the writer's vision and allowing the script to take visual form via their pencil, the writer's

Marvel Method script instead breathed life into the artist's vision with dialogue created to match the panel drawings. Although the writer's synopsis provided original inspiration for the penciled panels, it was the penciler who undertook the first permanent creative decisions in the issue's creation, arguably making them the primary writer for the issue's plot.

Upon examination of both the copied panels and the resulting scripts, it appears that Lee wrote these final scripts in two stages. Lee appears to often begin by writing notes in either pencil or pen—seemingly whatever instrument he had on hand—outside the margins of the panels with ideas for dialogue and narration.

Such marginalia are not universally present in edited pencils available in the Stan Lee Papers (see, for example, Romita Sr.);[26] in fact, this is the opposite of how marginalia's Marvel Method function is usually described. When describing how the Marvel Method works in the current comic industry, Brian Michael Bendis explains that "[a]s the artist breaks down the story [into pencils], he may jot down story notes or dialogue ideas in the margins of the art, hence *margin notes*" (Bendis 28, emphasis original). However, the marginalia I found in the Stan Lee Papers matches the hundreds of other examples of Lee's handwriting examples in the archive, and the majority of his notes do not seem to apply to other members of the creative team, instead suggesting potential dialogue. Rather than receiving notes written in the margins by his collaborators, Lee's marginal notes appear to be directed toward himself.

The use of margin notes by Lee rather than by his artistic cocreators, who would understandably have needed to communicate their decision-making process to him, suggests that this note-taking operates as a site of possible variation from the original synopsis (which, as previously explained, was not commonly available in the archive) or that this note-taking was done on separate and since-discarded sheets of paper.

In the second stage, Lee would use a thick, usually black marker to draw on top of the copied pencils to note how he envisioned the composition of speech bubbles and narration boxes while also writing the official script. In the Stan Lee Papers, these scripts match the length of the newly created artwork, with one typewritten page for each page of the comic. While Lee's final script usually follows the notes he made on his copy of the penciled panels, there are still instances in the archive showing that his initial script notes were not set in stone. On his penciled copy of *The Mighty Thor* #385, his notes for the second page indicate Lee initially considered the interaction between the Hulk and random passers-by to be one of instant mutual hate, with the civilians debating calling the police when they discover the Hulk and the green behemoth (reasonably) angered at their fear-driven response. In his typed script, however, the final dialogue depicts the passers-by as horrified not by the Hulk, whom they cannot see, but by the destruction of the (former) forest around them, wondering what could have possibly caused this. Then the Hulk, who had been concealed from the onlookers (and based on Lee's note to editor Ralph Macchio in the script, from the readers)[27] under a pile of tree trunks, wakes up and begins a rampage (S. Lee, *Thor Special*).[28] Although Jim Shooter, not Lee, was responsible for creating the issue's initial synopsis, the radical changes between the marginalia notes and the final dialogue show that even to its last possible iteration, Lee's ideas as a writer were mutable.

Inking/Coloring

Possibly due to the lack of Lee's involvement at this stage of the Marvel Method, there are few examples of comics in the inking and coloring stage found in the Stan Lee Papers. Most examples of these steps in the archive are partially inked pencils such as the one previously discussed or published issues. There seems to be little to learn about the later parts of the Marvel Method from examining the Lee archive.

However, upon comparing some Marvel Method artifacts with their published counterparts, there seems to be at least one instance in which Lee may not have been attributed for his creative contribution. In Box 51, Folder 12, there are multiple draft stages from the final installment of the two-issue annual series *Heroes and Legends* (published November 1997). While the issue's plot synopsis was written by James Felder, there is a typed page of dialogue and narration in the Stan Lee Papers (Felder; Lee, *Heroes and Legends: "Avengers Assemble!"*). While these script pages do not have an author's name, they do have various edits written in pen that resemble Lee's handwriting. In comparing this script to the final issue, it becomes clear that this was the version used for publication. However, the published issue does not include Lee as a credited creator.

This is particularly puzzling. If this is indeed an instance in which Lee's work is unattributed, it is unclear why Marvel Comics would omit his name from official creator credits. Even when he transitioned to a chairman emeritus position the next year, Lee was often cited on the covers of comics in which he had little involvement so that the issue could draw more sales (Raphael and Spurgeon 251), so it would not be a matter of discounting Lee's contributions. It is definitely not because Marvel wished to limit the number of collaborators on the cover, as eight of the issue's contributors are listed underneath the title.[29]

I have no logical explanation regarding why this happened, but this does imply that Lee may have been involved as a writer or editor in other Marvel projects. It is possible there are numerous other instances in which Lee's creative contributions have been obscured.

Conclusion: Assigning Credit

When discussing the history of superhero comics, it is easy to fall into the simplistic thinking often found in superheroes' earliest iterations: that there is a black-and-white dichotomy in its players, that the people who were involved in their creation can also be categorized as valorous heroes or dastardly villains, and that there is some straightforward and surefire way of determining which is which. I made the same mistake, beginning my research for this chapter enthusiastically prepared to lambast Lee as a man who diminished the contributions of his cocreators to increase his own status. But as this chapter demonstrates, the truth is much more complicated. After moving past popular reputation and generalities to the archival evidence in the University of Wyoming's Stan Lee Papers, it becomes clear that the Marvel Method that is described by comics professionals in industry explainers and how-to books does not describe its everyday enactment during the time that Lee worked at Marvel Comics. It also becomes clear that if the Marvel Method as it was prescribed creates a working relationship that relies on pencilers taking on many if not most writing functions, the enacted Marvel Method creates even more potential for unacknowledged authorial contributions even as it obscures the true origin of these additions.

Just as the Marvel Method process is more complex upon closer examination, so is Lee's standing as a major figure who popularized this process. Stan Lee's status in the context of the acknowledgment of his collaborators and cocreators is ambiguous. It is reasonable to say that Lee's name was credited to writing decisions that were not truly his; if such a thing were to happen with a writer working today, they would understandably be called a plagiarist. But in his twentieth-century context, working within a publishing industry that had been silently propping up a character's originators through series of ghostwriters and ghostartists, Lee can be seen as something of an early champion of multiple authorship in comics. The Marvel Method he helped popularize allowed the artists he worked with to embellish their own ideas, creating a space in which they could freely create. In multiple statements targeted at comic book fans and to general public, Lee explicitly said that creating comics was, by nature, a collaborative exercise. When the previous paradigm was to deny artistic credit, any attempt at proper attribution is a large leap toward fairness.

That said, sectioning his cocreators into strictly defined roles—writer, penciler, etc.—did not fully encapsulate what each person brings to the finished product in any comic book, much less in the Marvel Method, in which many traditional writing decisions are made by the penciler. While the Marvel Method draft documents in the Stan Lee Papers are not as complete as one may like—there is a surprising lack of synopses, the only document where we can be relatively sure that the ideas were Lee's and Lee's alone—it is clear that the people who worked with Lee had even more creative license than they would have through the traditional script process. But it is also evident that we will never truly know the extent of their contributions to the final product, and by extension the legacy that is now Marvel Comics.

Traditional Process	Marvel Method
1. Editor and writer discuss ideas.	1. Writer and editor discuss ideas.*
2. Writer creates pitch.	2. Writer creates 1–2-page synopsis.
3. Editor approves pitch.	3. Editor approves synopsis.
4. Writer writes script with action, dialogue, and possibly panel layout suggestions.	4. Penciler takes synopsis and creates drawings for full-length comic.
5. Editor approves script, gives script to penciler.	5. Writer takes pencils and creates script with dialogue and narration.
6. Penciler draws panels using script.	6. Inker inks in pencils.
7. Editor approves penciled drawings ("pencils"), gives pencils to inker.	7. Colorist selects colors.
8. Inker goes over pencils with ink.	8. Letterer adds dialogue bubbles, narration boxes, etc.
9. Editor gives inked drawings to letterer and colorist.	9. Editor approves coloring and lettering.
10. Colorist selects colors.	10. Final product sent to press.
11. Letterer adds dialogue bubbles, narration boxes, etc.	
12. Editor approves colors and lettering.	*Note: During the time that Stan Lee was actively involved in creating comics, he was often both writer and editor.
13. Final product sent to press.	

CHAPTER 3

WHICH EARTH IS THIS AGAIN?
The Retcon vs. The Multiverse

Introduction

The previous two chapters examined collaborative authorship and its function in comics in the context of projects with clearly delineated timescales—either a limited miniseries such as Moore, Gibbons, and Higgins's *Watchmen,* or the process Stan Lee and his various cocreators used to create individual issues using the Marvel Method. While these focused chapters have been useful for the purposes of (re)constructing how collaborative authorship works on the level of single teams working towards a short-term collaborative goal, their purposefully circumscribed topics do not allow for an understanding of the full scope of how collaborative authorship operates within the larger superhero comics industry. The majority of superhero comics are not created as stand-alone issues or limited series, but as part of long-term productions sometimes spanning generations—both in terms of creative teams and decades. Therefore, to think of superhero comics solely in terms of short-term creative projects undergone by a single collaborative team in effect denies the larger realities of the genre and its creative and publication practices. Instead, there is much to gain from examining how collaborative authorship in mainstream superhero comics operates on a much longer timescale and analyzing the strategies that superhero comics franchises have utilized to manage complex systems of collaborative creation through the complex balancing of narrative strategies.

Never-ending Stories and the Rise of Continuity

In terms of sheer time, the mainstream comics industry encapsulates what may arguably be the longest-running collaborative writing projects in history. Superman, the oldest superhero published by "the Big Two," was first featured in *Action Comics* #1 in May 1938 (Siegel and Shuster),[1] a series that has been published on a near-monthly basis ever since and published its thousandth issue in April 2018 with no signs of stopping (Garcia-López et al.). Other superstar superheroes are not far behind, with DC Comics publishing eightieth anniversary commemorative issues for Batman, Robin, and the Joker since then (Levitz and Erickson; Wielgosz et al.; Woodard et al.).

This seemingly unending storytelling marathon would be next to impossible if singular authorship were the norm for these comics; one creator would naturally tire, physically and/or mentally, of such long-running projects. Even taking into account that both the nominal writer and nominal artist can functionally act as cowriters, as seen in the two previous chapters, to expect any single creative team to produce material for a single series for decades is daunting to even conceive.

Therefore, it is uncommon to have the same creators throughout the entire run of a long-term series. Instead, such endeavors typically entail constantly evolving sets of creators moderated by the controlling companies. Each of these creative teams—often assigned by the company, though on occasion hand-chosen by a writer whose pitch has been approved—typically works together to produce issues for a set amount of time and is then replaced by the succeeding team, stepping down to (hopefully) be reassigned to other titles. With every new consecutive team taking up where the previous one left off, a comic book series might be best conceived as a long-running collaborative project in which most of its contributors never communicate with their coauthors despite their shared creation in a forever-unfinished project.

But even taking into account the long-term collaborative project of a continuous series belies the actual complexity of the industry's collaborative storytelling. If any comic book reader were to make a trip to a local comic book store and browse the new-release section that is often on prominent display, it becomes plain that popular superheroes are rarely confined to a single series. As of July–August 2020, Marvel Comics' Peter Parker, aka Spider-Man, was the protagonist in five currently ongoing series: *The Amazing Spider-Man, Amazing Spider-Man: Daily Bugle, Spider-Man: Noir, Spider-Man,* and *Symbiote Spider-Man: Alien Reality* ("List of Current Marvel Comics Publications"). This count does not include simultaneously published series featuring the beloved web-slinger's friends, in which he likely makes regular appearances (e.g., *The Amazing Mary Jane, Miles Morales: Spider-Man, Spider-Woman, Gwen Stacy*), or any random encounters depicted in any other Marvel title (which may range from a single-panel cameo in the background to a multi-issue superhero team-up).

In the early years of comic book publishing, there was no expectation that these stories would affect one another. When comic books were being sold on newsstands, there was no way to guarantee vendors would consistently stock each issue of any series, much less multiple series starring the same character. Comic book companies could not presume that their readers would be able to get consecutive issues in a series or several issues from multiple series (Pearson and Uricchio 28–29). These conditions directly discouraged continuity and engendered looser expectations regarding how stories and characters were treated by comic book creators than the ones that exist in the industry today. While there were some standard guidelines regarding treatment of a character—for example, nothing that could "tarnish the character's brand and stayed within the basic confines of his established personality" (Friedenthal 89–90)—superheroes did not progress linearly (or, some may argue, at all) from story to story. The stories told in one issue would not affect those shown in another. Although the issues were numbered for publication and sales purposes, these tales of superheroism were told in isolation from one another and with no regard for chronology or continuity outside of the individual story.

Having such self-contained stories prohibited the linear progression of most serial installments but granted these early superhero tales a sense of existing outside the normal confines of time. As Umberto Eco argues in his essay "The Myth of Superman," Superman and the other superheroes from before the Marvel Age exist outside of the normal flow of time (Eco 150). Seeing the lack of continuity as a means of avoiding the ramifications of aging and death for these commercial characters,[2] Eco suggests that superhero comics' avoidance of continuity between Superman stories creates "a kind of oneiric climate—of which the reader is not aware at all—where what has happened before and what has happened after appear extremely hazy" (Eco 153). While issues were numbered for publication purposes, the individual stories (e.g., "the time Superman fought a robot") could be told in any order without affecting one another, much like the tales of other, more classical heroes (e.g., "the time Odysseus fooled the Cyclops"), lending them a mythopoetic quality that offsets the static nature of these plots.

However, while this characterization describes the temporal situation of Golden Age comics, "even when his essay was published in 1972, Eco's argument was not quite up-to-date with then-current superhero comics" (Kukkonen 48), due to changes in the marketing and sales of comic books. In response to declining comics sales at newspaper stands, comic book publishers had increasingly turned to the direct market, in which comics appear in specialized shops that buy comics through the publisher's designated distributor. In this model, store operators "adopted an inventory burden by ordering titles from distributors on non-returnable terms based on perception of consumer demand in their niche market" (Johnson 79). Although comic book companies had been in competition with one another on newsstand shelves, specialty stores were making a gamble with each issue they displayed, intensifying the rivalry.

Such a sales environment led to a number of new marketing techniques in order to gain advantage in the cutthroat race to cover specialty shop shelves. Marvel Comics "dominated the niche direct market, [but] competition from DC Comics as well as several new indie publishers appealing to alternative tastes collectively threatened its market share. Given that direct market retailers only ordered as many comics as they thought they could sell in a finite market, Marvel saw a zero sum game where every competitor's sale meant one less potential Marvel sale" (Johnson 84). To try to manipulate the market to their favor, Marvel began to feature popular characters across multiple issues simultaneously and thereby "forced readers to choose: get the full experience by spending more or all of their comic budget on [all of the books depicting their favorite characters, such as] *X-Men* titles, or spend on the competition and miss out" (Johnson 84).

Part of the impetus to collect all simultaneously printed issues with a particular character was also due to another change in superhero comics: the increased connectedness between printed issues in the form of multi-issue story arcs. Although newsstand distribution did not support multi-issue story arcs, the direct market did. If a newsstand reader was only made aware of a story arc upon the release of the story's continuing issues, they would have no way to access these previously published issues, which would have likely been returned to the newsstand distributor to make room for the new issue. Unless a friend happened to have the previous issues of that story, the reader would find themselves *in medias res* in a plot told linearly, leading to frustration and confusion. However, with the direct market, a store's unsold inventory is typically not given back, but stored in the back issues section for an interested customer to find. Therefore, discovering an interesting story at any time after its first installment does not prohibit enjoyment of the complete story being told in full.

This increased use of multi-issue arcs assisted the comic book companies in two complementary ways. First, it created an "interest in the unsold back issues held by retailers at a potential loss" (Johnson 79) as readers searched to get complete stories for their collection, because missing an issue would be something akin to reading a book with five chapters that lacked, for example, chapter 3. Such back-issue sales boosted the profile of a title for retailers, who would possibly continue to order the series due to its popularity (and therefore the guarantee that any issues the stores bought would sell).

Second, and perhaps more importantly, dedicated readers, once they found an enjoyable story in a favorite genre, would often dedicate themselves to reading the story all of the way through "to find out how it ends"; as the more traditional literary market shows, this remains true even across multiple novel-length installments. If a comic book reader discovered a captivating story arc early—perhaps, if they were lucky, with the first issue—the reader was nearly guaranteed to purchase the story arc's remaining issues.

While this connection from issue to issue within a comic book series was initially only between a story arc's installments, this gradually morphed into a longer-term continuity from story arc to story arc. As Eco notes, "*[b]efore* causally determines *after*" (Eco 150, emphasis original), suggesting that any comic book issues that occur in chronological relation to another opens up the possibility that all of these story arcs occur subsequently as well, something that would "turn mere comic books into chronicles of alternate histories" (Morrison 114). In combination with various practices that rewarded readers for finding inconsistencies between stories, such as Marvel Comics' infamous No-Prize,[3] comic book fans not only began to look for continuity between character appearances throughout their fictional universe, but formed "a niche market in which loyalty and continuity would be assumed" (Johnson 79) by comic book companies, creators, and consumers. Continuity between series and between story arcs is now considered common practice in the world of superhero comics.

A Tangled Web: Continuity and Its Discontents

Although continuity has the above-noted benefits of boosting sales and creating customer loyalty to a particular series if not the company's entire fictional universe, it comes with its own problems. In long-running series, particularly those published by larger comics publishers, a standard expectation of continuity creates several disadvantages both theoretical and practical that compound with the ever-lengthening existence of a character and its popularity.

First, there is the logistical problem of progression through time. Even though individual stories no longer appear in and as isolated bubbles of time, time still does not operate in comic books as it does in real life. With few notable exceptions—such as the Marvel Comics trend of "Old Man [insert character here]" miniseries[4] and DC Comics' John Constantine, who celebrated his fortieth birthday in the sixty-third issue in his titular series (Ennis et al.)—superhero comics are consistently depicted as the same age as when they made their debut, no matter how long ago that was. While typically an unstated amount of time passes between story arcs much like those Eco describes, the advancement of time in comics still breaks down upon examination, as a character's continued viability requires them to never age.

Conversely, while even supposedly mortal characters in superhero comics are seemingly immune to the effects of aging, time still moves around them. Comics, like all popular media, must remain relevant to maintain their popularity. Since for the most part superhero comics are set in a present much like "real life," the worlds around these characters are constantly changing to reflect the contemporaneous world, though the characters progress at a much slower rate. Despite having in some cases literally decades' worth of adventures, characters like Barry Allen (aka the second Flash) are still roughly the same age whether changing costumes in a (now extremely rare) phone booth or texting on a cell phone.

However, as continuity has become normalized from comics to non-superhero genres, multiple approaches to this conundrum have emerged. Some follow the notion of what TV Tropes calls "Comic-Book Time," also called the "sliding" or "floating" timescale: that all comics are moving through the illusion of time, but that any given time occurs always-already in the present ("Comic-Book Time"). An altogether different, almost Eco-ist approach is to flout all notions of linear time in comic books. When Grant Morrison was asked at the 2010 San Francisco Comic-Con the exact age of Bruce Wayne (aka Batman) and Robin,[5] the famed Batman writer told the fan: "It doesn't matter. You must understand that these people aren't real. I'm like, Batman's a mythical figure. I'm being funny but I'm not being funny because they don't live in the real world. [. . .] So basically Batman is 75 years old and Robin is 74 years old but they never grew old, because they're different from us. They're paper people, okay?" (DC Comics).

No matter which approach is taken, time in superhero comics quickly becomes achronological, and even more so upon close examination. It is only through collective agreement between creators and readers to ignore the ever-changing present that flows past these decades-old, nonaging characters or to forgo the question of continuity that the current expectation for continuity in superhero comics can be satisfied.

Second, from a storytelling perspective, an additional wrinkle to the smooth progression of continuity entails the question of character growth. Before comic book readers had any expectation of continuity, a character did not take new knowledge and experience from one adventure to another; rather than being dynamic, growing and changing, a character was "an archetype, the totality of certain collective aspirations" (Eco 149). The enjoyment of the story came not from watching a character grow from experience to experience, but from the outlandishness of the situations the character found itself in and the ultimate victory. But now that issues and series are perceived as explicitly or implicitly connected to one another, having such a static nature is no longer acceptable. A character's actions now have an impact that carries beyond the bounds of a single printed issue, and that must be taken into account by its creators.

Continuity and character growth also bring the danger of too rapid progression. When stories were disconnected from one another with no expectation of continuity, a superhero's powers could appear and disappear without notice. However, if readers now expect superhero stories to now have lasting consequences for a character, then they will also expect a superhero to be able to display new skills when their adventures require it. While adding a new ability to a character's superhuman arsenal can be exciting and may draw in new, interested readers, they pose the further danger of what the video gaming community has termed "power creep," or "the phenomenon by which content becomes completely worthless" (Everett).

Older characters who became established long before the introduction of comics continuity are particularly prone to this problem, with Jerry Siegel and Joe Shuster both admitting that their creation, Superman, is a classic victim of this phenomenon (Daniels, *DC Comics: A Celebration of the World's Favorite Comic Book Heroes* 26). In the character's inception, Superman's increased strength allowed him to jump incredibly high, allowing him to "leap tall buildings in a single bound," as the 1940–51 radio series boasted in its opening lines (Beck et al.). However, this changed in 1941, when the Fleischer Studios animated films depicted him as flying (Cronin, "Comic Book Legends Revealed #373"). Such a dramatic change, which was made to simplify animation and to better fit the new medium's aesthetics, would likely not be allowed now, with today's raised expectations of consistency between depictions of Superman. But in the 1940s, DC

Comics was not concerned with continuity, and with a few, steadfast exceptions, Superman writers were only bound to what pop culture fans often refer to as "the rule of cool": if a story decision would be interesting or fun, then all liberties taken with a character or plot were forgiven. Thus Superman no longer just leapt over buildings, he could fly over them as well. Similar backstories can be given for the majority of Superman's powers: laser vision, ice breath, super-senses, etc. But what is notable or useful about the ability to jump, no matter how far, when one can fly? In addition, although the emphasis on continuity allows for characters to evolve over time, it also limits potential modification of these characters for fear of rendering them too powerful to use outside of *deus ex machina* scenarios.

On the practical side, creating long-running series with an expectation of continuity also creates a number of concerns for creators and readers alike. As noted previously in this section, a series that becomes popular will be assigned to a number of consecutive creative teams, and popular characters will likely be featured in numerous appearances in other series. Each time a character comes under the control of new creators, that new creative team's contributions take part in a protracted discourse with previous (and possibly future) creative teams. They are responding, in one shape or form, to what came before; assuming that the character and storyworld continue to be published after the current creators move on, their successors will respond in some fashion to the current contributions.

But like the change of speakers in any conversation, this new set of contributions requires a delicate balancing act between upholding a sense of what came before and introducing something new. When control over a work or character is transferred to another, the subsequent creator is usually compelled, "above all, to prove that he was able to do as good a job as [the original creator(s)] while also doing something different" (Baetens 37). On one hand, this new version must be similar enough to previous ones that fans will continue to purchase the title. If a character or their adjacent themes (truth and justice for Superman, power and responsibility for Spider-Man, etc.) are too dramatically altered, the things that made these characters and stories initially appealing will become unrecognizable and readers will take their comic book money to more enjoyable titles.

On the other hand, nobody enjoys chiming into a conversation just for their contribution to be judged utterly unnoteworthy. Similarly, creators also often feel the need to make their heroes distinct so that they will be memorable. As Jackson Ayres notes, "How these creators approached joining an ongoing series expressed the logics of their authorial selves" (Ayres 241). When a suitably distinctive take on the character becomes popular enough, it achieves a mark of distinction among comic book fans, other creators, and company executives that will attach to both creators and characters for the rest of their careers, encouraging not only further popularity but also more means to take creative license. If a creator can create a definitive new take on a character—for example, Matt Fraction and David Aja's Hawkeye (2012–15), Grant Morrison et al.'s Batman (2006–13), etc.—which is favorably remembered years after their run has ended, then their future career in the fast-churning world of comic book publishing is vastly more assured.

But this balancing act becomes more and more precarious with each successive changeover. If continuity were to remain unbroken and unchanged, creators would have to accommodate each previous version, down to their finest details with each new iteration. This is, of course, an increasingly daunting task the longer a title or character exists, and even with editors dedicated to the task of maintaining continuity, "mistakes" happen; "inconsistencies emerg[e] in the different storylines and encounters involving these characters, and continuity" (Kukkonen 40). Even in a perfect environment, where creators are experts in every panel of a character's history, each writing decision reduces the pool of future possibilities. In an environment in which readers have been conditioned to pounce on inconsistencies, the simple advancement of time becomes a threat to the maintenance of a single, consistent continuity. Although the introduction of continuity encouraged readers to make regular trips to the niche-specialty comic shops in order to not be left behind, "the coherent and consistent development of the characters and their storyworlds, bec[ame] a problem" as storylines developed over time (Kukkonen 40).

The presumption that readers will be able to notice these inconsistencies, however, is founded on another one: that readers of these comic books have been doing so since a character's inception. This is an unreasonable assumption. As movies and TV shows have increasingly taken inspiration from superhero comics, new readers are being generated every day. With these media adaptations now turning to less well-known properties for new content, even lifelong fans of the genre are discovering (or rediscovering) characters they want to learn more about by reading their original content. But if characters and their storyworlds have been continuously developing since their first appearance, where should a new reader begin? When a potential new reader enters a comic store for the first time and tells an employee they saw *Shazam!* last week and want to start reading about him in the comics, should they be told to begin with his first-ever appearance in *Whiz Comics* #2, published in 1939 by Fawcett Comics (DC Comics purchased the license for the character in the 1972 and purchased it outright in 1994 [Cronin, "Comic Book Urban Legends Revealed #12!"]), or should they begin with the issues published this year, potentially missing important background that colors a character's present interaction with their storyworld? Long-running series can be cumbersome for new readers, as they would need to read years—in some cases, decades—of backstory before being able to understand currently published issues. Potential comic book readers will perhaps choose to find different ways to spend their time and money—ones not requiring potentially thousands of pages of "homework" for full enjoyment. Time and continuity, once again, become a double-edged sword that both encourage current readers and potentially scare away new ones.

However, these problems are not ultimately fatal to the superhero comics industry; if they were, the narrative structure of these vast storyworlds would have collapsed under their own weight decades ago. Over time, creators in the genre have used two methods of enabling the telling of new stories: retroactive continuity (also called the retcon) and the use of multiverses.

Revise/Reboot: The Retcon

As outlined above, expecting an absolutely continuous and consistent story over the course of decades and potentially several creative teams is unreasonable at best and increasingly impossible at worst. As time progresses, a character or storyworld's publication history becomes more and more tenuously balanced upon itself, threatening the integrity of the storyworld's internal logic and verisimilitude. But with this conundrum comes its own potential solution: if it is history of the fictional character or world that is hindering its further development, then perhaps that history can be revised or reconceived in favor of the current creative team's intentions and needs. It is through this logic that retroactivity continuity changes, often shortened to "retcons," have come to fruition.

The idea of revising past stories to fit a new present is itself not new. In the sole scholarly work on the subject, Andrew J. Friedenthal points to the Old Testament's Book of Genesis (which tells two different versions of how God created the Earth and humans) to suggest that this technique likely began with oral storytelling, predating the use of writing (15). But although the concept of retroactive continuity changes predated superhero comics and has since spread throughout long-running popular media, the term was first coined in superhero comics. As part of their revival of *All-Star Squadron* (original run 1940–51, revival 1976–78), Roy Thomas, Arvell Jones, and Mike Clark continued where the original 1940–51 run left off, setting the series firmly within the Golden Age of comics and in the past for characters within other DC Comics storylines. This temporal displacement was apparently noticed by readers, who discussed this with Thomas both in letters and at conventions. In the letters section of *All-Star Squadron* #18,[6] Thomas officially names this in response to a fan letter: "As for what Roy himself (myself) is trying to do, we like to think an enthusiastic *ALL-STAR* booster at one of Adam Malin's Creation Conventions in San Diego came up with the best name for it, a few months back: '**Retroactive Continuity**.' Has kind of a ring, don't you think?" R.T. (Thomas et al. 26, emphasis original)

The idea of "retroactive continuity," and its more popular shortening "retcon," is now accepted by the majority of comic book fans for all changes to past continuity and is now considered a major component of storytelling in the world of superhero comics.

The retcon has become such an engrained aspect of storytelling in comic books, in fact, that it can be explicitly invoked within the comic book storyworld. In the limited series *Symbiote Spider-Man: Alien Reality*, Dr. Stephen Strange and Spider-Man discover that the supervillain Hobgoblin has stolen a magical book called the *Word of God* that allowed him and his partner-in-crime Baron Mordo to rewrite reality. Once he learns through clairvoyance that the duo has erased the book from history, the Sorcerer Supreme explains to Spider-Man:

> STRANGE: You don't understand—Mordo didn't just destroy it. He *undid* it. He used it to rewrite history one final time. He wiped its own existence out of reality so that it was never inscribed in the first place.
> SPIDER-MAN: So basically you're saying he retconned it.
> STRANGE: All right, now *I* have no idea what *you're* talking about.
> SPIDER-MAN: *Retroactive continuity*. It was a phrase mentioned in the letters page in of a comic book and was shortened to retcon. It means you rewrite history to match up with the present. (David et al. 7, emphasis original)

Given how accepted a practice the retcon has become in superhero comics, it is unsurprising that not all retcons function to the same degree or manner. As Friedenthal notes, these alterations can take a number of forms, many of which have been exhaustingly listed by media enthusiasts at the meta-analysis website TVTropes.com under tongue-in-cheek names like "Remember the New Guy?" or "Backported Development" (7–8; "TV Tropes"), and such minute analysis could be the subject of an entire book unto itself. But that does not mean that retcons cannot be analyzed under broader categorizations. While they are referred to by the same collective term, upon closer inspection it becomes clear that retcons can largely be divided into two major subcategories, which I will call "soft" and "hard" retcons.

Revising History: The Soft Retcon

In terms of retroactively altering continuity, the soft retcon acts much like a revision; it makes smaller alterations to an established present. These often take the form of presenting new information about past events to characters in the storyworld—for instance, in the 2004–6 Batman "Under the Red Hood" story arc, we learn that former Robin Jason Todd, who had died at the hands of the Joker in the infamous 1988 *Death in the Family* arc, had been secretly alive for years and returned to Gotham under the alias The Red Hood (Starlin et al.; Winick et al.)—or in the form of a flashback that adds new context to a past interaction between characters.

No matter which specific form these revisions take, all soft retcons serve the same purpose of remolding the past by adding, removing, or otherwise altering the already established information to better serve the current story. When Jason Todd was revealed to be The Red Hood, the majority of Batman continuity was not upended. The events within *Death in the Family* remained part of the established canon, as do most of those that took place afterward. However, this retcon went back to alter one fact—that Jason Todd remained dead after he was buried—thereby opening the narrative to new possibilities.

In terms of storytelling, these soft retcons are the easiest to use because they are the most conservative way to enact desired changes. Although comic book creators and readers take positions all over the political spectrum, decades of comic book publication have led them to expect a consistent continuity, resulting in a certain, non-political conservative antagonism towards large changes. With soft retcons, creators do not need to throw away most of an established history but merely revise the facts and stories that were established by the creators before them. Additionally, these new changes may be carried forward by future creative teams, possibly leaving an impact on the course of the story for years to come.

Let's Start Over: The Hard Retcon

Hard retcons are far less common but have a much more intense impact on the comics canon. If the purpose of a soft retcon is to preserve as much of the established canon as possible through precise revisions of our understanding of the past, then the purpose of a hard retcon is to wipe the slate clean. It is a complete reboot, in which creators can throw away the trappings of the past and rebuild a character from the ground up. This is often done to retell origin stories in a newer context, such as modernizing the origins of characters conceived early in the twentieth century to fit the tastes of contemporary audiences. While soft retcons are a regular occurrence within superhero comics and appear on a regular basis, hard retcons are so rare that such events are often given notice in periodicals and public-interest journals not dedicated to the subject of comics.

These produce extreme alterations to continuity, so much so that Friedenthal does not see reboots as a form of retcon, because he sees them as coming not from "a part of the story world," but from a "marketing decision imposed from the outside" (Friedenthal 7). But while Friedenthal is correct that most soft retcons are given in-world explanations, these changes do not actually come from within; all plot and its attendant continuity, whether maintained or altered through retcons, are decisions made by creators and the controlling companies that employ them. These changes are made *to* the storyworld, not by it; therefore, the distinction between whether they are given in-universe explanations or not is somewhat arbitrary. Similarly, both the revising and rebooting of what is currently considered canonical in the comics (at least, until the next retcon) "involves the revisiting of past stories, told in previous installments of a long-form narrative, and adding a new piece of information to that older story, literally rewriting the past" (Friedenthal 6). It is merely a matter of degree of change and frequency of use.

As reboots function by starting canonicity anew and rendering all previous continuity invalid, such hard retcons are used sparingly, typically as a way to "restart" an entire comics universe at once. Although they are much rarer than soft retcons, hard retcons/reboots still have distinct advantages over their soft counterparts. First, they allow for more radical alterations of a character. Perhaps a creator has proposed a new, interesting idea of how to use a character that, while intriguing, is incompatible with the character as currently conceived; or perhaps readers are tired of a particular character, and it needs a profound makeover to regain or maintain its former appeal. While soft retcons make smaller, more gradual changes to a character, in a reboot, creators can transform it into something totally new—provide a new backstory, adjust its powers to be more interesting, or even give it completely new personality traits—without having to build a transition from one to another or provide an in-world explanation for these changes. The continuity is dead; long live the continuity.

Second, hard retcons can act as equalizers among comics readers. Because comics continuity is constantly changing, it can become increasingly difficult to keep track of all that is currently canonical; while there are a number of printed guidebooks to help newer readers learn more about these vast storyworlds, they can quickly become outdated through the use of both soft and hard retcons. Among comic fans a lot of cultural capital is to be gained by anyone who can maintain—and keep updated—vast mental schema that accommodate these never-ending changes as well as all previous iterations. This, however, disadvantages newer readers or those who do not have the time or money to access (i.e., to purchase and read) the vast number of back issues required to do this. A reboot helps level this playing field, allowing old and new readers alike to begin again on the same page, literally and metaphorically.

Hard retcons can also entice new readers. Due to the vast comprehensiveness of continuity, superhero comics have gained a reputation its complicated lore, and an understanding of the past comics canon has become "an essential aspect of both the consumption and enjoyment" (Miettinen 6); therefore, a wide-ranging reset of comics canon like that of the hard retcon is a rare event and opportunity. Announcements of complete-universe reboots, like that of DC Comics' New 52 revamp and relaunch in 2011 that aimed to revamp "the serial continuity of DC's whole multiverse" (Stein 1), are big news, likely to be commented upon even in newspapers and magazines that are not dedicated to comics. This publicity, essentially announcing to potential readers that one of the greatest barriers to fully enjoying superhero comics has recently been reduced to its lowest level, can bring in new readers, who will then (these companies hope) stay with the stories as they again build up to their previous levels of continuity complexity.

Forgetting to Forget: The Limitations of Retcons

Although soft and hard retcons have their own uses, they do have many similar disadvantages. First, any effort to revise or completely erase the past is limited in its power to effect change. Just because comic books creators write events or information into or out of existence does not mean that those cease to exist both in print and in memory. To quote the Symbiote Spider-Man, "the thing with retcons is, they aren't real. People always remember. *Always*" (David et al. 8, emphasis original). Whether or not current continuity acknowledges information retconned away, that information persists both on the previously published page and in the memory of the reader. My stating that the previous sentence is invalid does not change the fact that you remember it, or that you can still go back and read it. While readers may be able to make room for newly revealed information, the entire readership is unlikely to forget previously canonical information merely at the will of a new creative team. Even hard retcons, therefore, do not erase the past; they merely indicate which aspects of the past canon the current creative team wishes readers to ignore.

Of course, this signaling can only be effective if there is complete adherence on the part of the readership. For a reader to alter their knowledge of continuity to reflect a retcon, they must first read the issue in which these changes occur. With the exception of pandemic-level publication disruptions, dozens of superhero comic books are typically released every week, costing up to (and sometimes above) $5 apiece. Comic book readers, like everyone else, have other demands on their time and money; even dedicated fans can find it difficult to keep up. Even if all comic book fans automatically accepted all continuity changes as the new canon—which, as described in the final chapter, rarely occurs—it cannot be guaranteed that every single comic book reader will read every single comic book, particularly if they are fans of multiple characters. Although fan groups on social media and other dedicated websites may help fill in gaps in reading, it is still possible for fans to miss soft retcons or be unaware of the finer differences between hard retcons. Any given comic book reader's understanding of continuity can vary wildly from another's due to simple accidents of infrequent or incomplete readership, throwing the idea of mass continuity into a state of "textual anarchy" (Miettinen 5). Therefore, while the creative team may be responsible for creating the retcon, that retcon's effective reinterpretation or reinscription of past continuity depends on the dedication and scope of a particular issue's readership.

This problem of retcons requiring a completely knowledgeable readership extends to successive creators. When a comic book title receives a new creator, these creators are rarely knowledgeable about all intricacies of a character's past continuity, and once hired are expected to produce on a deadline. While they may be provided with the highlights of a character's history—whether through examples or through summaries—publishing companies do not expect creators to know everything that has occurred in past continuity. In addition to having their own ideas regarding characterization and plot, creators, like readers, have knowledge gaps; they may simply not know of a softer retcon that occurred years ago. Therefore, many comic book fans treat an incoming new writer (who, due to their official title, is largely given credit for writing-related decisions, regardless of any possible contribution by other members of the creative team) as the portent of an unofficial soft retcon; until the readers have a sense of how this new creator will approach the title, all facts established by previous writers are up for potential reinterpretation.

Finally, the frequency itself of retcons, particularly harder retcons, can incur negative effects. While one of the appealing factors of radically altering a character or a storyworld via a reboot is to create an easy starting point for new readers, this clean-slate approach can have negative effects on dedicated readers. For many long-time fans of the genre, the ever-building complexity of superhero continuities are part of the enjoyment, and they will spend large amounts of time, money, and mental energy building nearly encyclopedic knowledge of their favorite characters.[7] With such knowledge bases, small changes via revisions are much more easily accommodated than hard retcons, which can invalidate all those efforts. Even though clean-slate retcons have not turned off the majority of readers in the past, if such reboots occur too frequently, it becomes difficult for dedicated readers to reinvest themselves—in money for purchasing issues, in time spent reading, in mental effort recreating schema. If a storyworld resets itself every few years, why bother to become attached to any particular version? Readers are less likely to purchase comics if they believe issues they purchase will be rendered apocryphal in a few years, and fans who enjoyed particular versions may feel "abandoned" by a reboot (Gordon 11). Even mid-level fans—that is, relatively new readers who are nonetheless interested in going further back into the publication history than the most recent reboot—easily find themselves daunted by the number of changes to reorganize. The retcon, therefore, is a double-edged sword that both helps and hinders the viability of long-term readership.

Through the Looking Glass: The Multiverse

The multiverse strategy, however, takes an altogether different approach to creative variance. I have likened a soft retcon to a revision and a hard retcon to rebooting and starting afresh, but the multiverse strategy has its own metaphors built into its operation; i.e., alternate and parallel universes. In the field of physics, it is hypothesized that the world we live in is not the only one that exists. These universes may vary slightly—for example, a universe in which the only difference from this one is that Baskin-Robbins boasts 32 flavors of ice cream[8]—or so much so that "our wars have had different outcomes than the ones we know. Species that are extinct in our universe have evolved and adapted in others. In other universes, we humans may have become extinct" (Clark).

While the science in this universe has not proven or disproven the existence of such universes, superhero comics have embraced this theory to develop a network of "mutually incompatible realities" (Kukkonen 41). The idea of multiple universes (or multiverses, for short) within comics, was first established in DC Comics' 1961 *The Flash* #123, titled "Flash of Two Worlds," in which Barry Allen's superspeed accidentally "tore a gap in the vibratory shields separating . . . worlds" (Fox et al. 8) and teamed up with the original Flash from the Golden Age of Comics, Jay Garrick, who only existed on Barry Allen's Earth as a comic book character (Fox et al. 9).[9] Since then, the existence of a multiverse has become a foundational part of the broader cosmologies established by both Marvel Comics and DC Comics.

Although these publishers largely focus on a single part of the multiverse—Earth-616 for Marvel, Earth 0 for DC—the storyworlds of both companies support large multiverses that are proclaimed to house all possible Earths, including those published by their rival company.[10]

The concept of the multiverse functions altogether differently from that of the retcon. The retcon, in both its soft and hard forms, alters a single narrative, either through smaller edits or through invalidating previous iterations and beginning again. The retcon acts upon a single timeline. In contrast, the multiverse introduces completely new and alternative continuities existing alongside the established one. In the multiverse, radical changes can be introduced without altering or throwing away the past; all changes are equally valid but exist in alternate universes. The retcon replaces or alters older versions—acting as an "instead of"; the multiverse introduces simultaneously existing alternatives—acting as an "and."

In terms of facilitating long-term storytelling, the multiverse allows for possibilities soft and hard retcons simply do not. Multiverses allow creators to experiment with hard retcon–style changes while preserving previous continuity like a soft retcon. Although reboots allow for complete reimaginings of character, these hard retcons within the main storyline still require the remade characters to retain the traits and circumstances at the core of their characters: Batman will always fight crime in Gotham City following the murder of his parents, Spider-Man will always learn about power and responsibility following the death of Uncle Ben, etc. A multiverse strategy, however, allows for the transformation of characters in ways that would be impossible if restricted to a single narrative universe in which these foundational aspects must remain consistent. The multiverse provides an avenue for exploring possible divergences from these foundations, whether in terms of setting—as in DC Comics' Elseworlds imprint, which has published limited series depicting a nineteenth-century Batman chasing Jack the Ripper in Victorian Gotham (Augustyn et al.) and Superman's Kryptonian ship crash-landing on a collective farm in Soviet-era Ukraine (Millar et al.)—or in terms of character, such as *The Deadpool Killogy*, in which Deadpool goes on a mission to rid the multiverse of superheroes that ultimately culminates in *Deadpool Kills Deadpool*, a free-for-all with alternate-universe versions of himself, including but not limited to Ladypool, Dogpool, Beard of Beespool, and Pandapool (Bunn et al.).

These divergences are fresh and often attract the attention of readers, but few of these multiversal alternatives have the sustainability required to make them permanent reboots of the iconic characters. After all, there is only so much fresh material to be gained from a version of Deadpool who is also a dog; if such a change were made via a hard retcon, sooner rather than later a new reboot would be required to change Dogpool back to Deadpool, lest readers lose interest in the character altogether. However, Dogpool existing as a Deadpool from a parallel universe can mean that Dogpool and Deadpool can exist simultaneously without contradiction; one does not preclude the other. If creators and readers tire of Dogpool, he can return to his own corner of the limitless multiverse and leave our Deadpool relatively unaltered by the experience.

In most cases, characters from outside the main continuity rarely make prolonged appearances; they often return to their homes on alternate earths in short order, once the current super-crisis that forced a multiversal team-up is addressed. However, the existence of a multiverse can also make space for the publishing companies to perform reboots on a smaller scale. When Sony began producing Spider-Man movies in the early 2000s, Marvel Comics was aware that some filmgoers would want to learn more about the character by reading the source material; however, there was noted concern that, for the reasons outlined earlier in this chapter, the character's massive publication history would prove too daunting for these potential fans-in-making. While they could have performed a hard retcon for a clean restart, Marvel instead introduced an updated and "modern" new line of comics. This imprint—Ultimate Marvel, later dubbed "the Ultimates Universe"—did not seek to replace Marvel's more traditional storylines from Earth-616. Instead, the series that make up this imprint are set in Earth-1610[11] and reboot classic characters like Spider-Man and the Fantastic Four so they are beginning their superhero careers in the present.[12] From 2000 to 2015, when Marvel Comics ended their Ultimate Marvel line, Earth-1610 acted as a reboot in microcosm, a stepping stone in which new readers could become generally familiar with characters without the baggage of decades' worth of backstory before (Marvel hoped) they migrated to titles within the main Marvel universe.[13]

However, despite their utility in creating avenues for divergent storylines, they entail their own complication in terms of maintaining vast storytelling enterprises. First, unlike retcons, which overwrite each other, alternate universes exist simultaneously and sometimes (though not always) interact. The introduction of a new alternate universe is a permanent addition to the franchise's ever-expanding cosmos, a new branching set of narrative variables and possibilities that exists within the larger confines of the storytelling universe. Barring a brand-wide retcon that eliminates specific universes, the multiverse never contracts, only expands, creating a vast array of canons whose interconnections must be navigated. This includes instances in which superhero characters cross over into the universes of rival companies, whether briefly as in Marvel's May 2018 *Lockjaw* #4 when the titular character spends a single panel in a DC Comics universe (Kibblesmith et al. 15)[14] or in the more explicit crossovers described previously in this chapter. Whether or not DC and Marvel actively choose to acknowledge this, the acceptance of the multiverse strategy has permanently interlinked their respective storyworlds, creating a tangled mess of retcons and multiverses that seek to reconcile themselves with each other.

Second, this permanency of divergent storylines can lead to a mindboggling array of alternate timelines to keep track of, particularly for readers of characters that are more likely to interact with alternate-universe selves, like DC's the Flash (whose dimension-transgressing super-speed has been the center of many DC multiverse crossovers) or Spider-Man (who has encountered alternate-universe Spider-[Wo]Men on numerous occasions). Although this can be useful for creators wishing to riff off their predecessors without overly complicating the main storyline, this can be a mixed blessing for both consumers and producers alike.

For consumers, while the forever-propagating multiverse allows for a variety of content to enjoy, it can also test the mental limits of dedicated readers. While Kukkonen argues that readers "do not need to be a super-reader, mentally juggling the innumerable storyworlds of the multiverse, in order to read superhero comics" (Kukkonen 42), this approach only works with individual storylines. If these readers wish to expand into the larger canon of multiverses, alternate universes, and what-ifs, or if they want to discuss the differences between them with other fans, such mental juggling becomes more of a requirement. For example, if fans of Spider-Man wish to discuss the character's multiversal counterparts, they must be able to organize numerous versions of a character with similar names but divergent mythologies, such as Spider-Ham,[15] Spider-Ma'am,[16] and Spiders-Man.[17] Even veteran readers with decades of experience can have trouble remembering all of these multiversal permutations, causing large swaths of the multiverse to become conflated or abandoned by fans. In the end, the multiverse approach's advantages in propagating variation also acts as its disadvantage: the multiverse builds upon itself until it exceeds the bandwidth of even the most dedicated fans' mental archives.

From an industry perspective, this type of self-exhaustion acts as both advantage and disadvantage. The introduction of new multiversal possibilities, especially when portraying variations of popular characters, is a surefire method of drawing quick sales. Some amount of built-in obsolescence is encouraged; as retcons demonstrate, in order to stay new and fresh, old ideas must be occasionally discarded to replace new ones. However, too much turnover in a short timeframe might prematurely limit the marketing possibilities of a particular alternate universe. If major multiverse variants are introduced slowly, they might be drawn out over a longer period of time—e.g., multiple limited series like the *White Knight* Batman universe[18]—but introducing these variants too quickly might encourage readers to lose interest in them before their narrative (and thus marketing) possibilities can be fully explored.

Additionally, the industry itself appears ambivalent to the idea of obsolescence. Because continuity is a central aspect of the genre, it is often self-referential. Particularly in Marvel Comics, which more heavily relies on the multiverse strategy than DC Comics, alternate universes and the characters they contain have a tendency to reappear years after their universe has been seemingly abandoned by the publisher. While Marvel Comics stopped publishing the Ultimates universe in 2015, the Earth-1610 version of Reed Richards was reintroduced in 2019 as an antagonist in a *Venom* series (Cates et al.); similarly, Miguel O'Hara—the futuristic Spider-Man from the year 2099—had last seen publication in 1996 before his surprise appearance in the 2014–15 *Spider-Verse* event. Even if alternate parts of the multiverse are often set aside to allocate printing resources to new ones, it seems that publishers—especially Marvel—do not want readers to truly, completely forget them; after all, they could be utilized again in future plotlines. Instead, the companies seem to hold contradictory desires: they want readers to forget about "old" multiversal counterparts until it is convenient for the company that the readers remember, at which point readers ideally remember this once-abandoned alternate history perfectly. Thus, while the constant expansion of the multiverse could theoretically be used as a built-in vehicle for obsolescence, the genre's own insistence on self-reference makes such forgetting difficult.

Mash-up: The Multiversal Retcon

While I have spent this chapter analyzing the retcon and the multiverse as distinct strategies used to manage long-term collaborative creation, it is important to note that they do not *always* appear separately within superhero comics. There are, on occasion, hard retcons that rewrite the multiverse and reconfigure the franchise's cosmology, the most famous of these being DC's 1985–86 *Crisis on Infinite Earths* storyline. In an attempt to reconcile what DC editors felt to be "a confusing mess of contradictory narratives that was gruelingly inaccessible to new readers" (Friedenthal 73), the company used the *Crisis* storyline to merge the DC storyworld—which at the time was spread throughout a multiverse—into a single universe that would henceforth be referred to as the "DC Universe."[19] This integration of the multiverse acted as a hard retcon that "wiped away the pasts of all DC's characters" (Daniels, *DC Comics: A Celebration of the World's Favorite Comic Book Heroes* 190) existing in separate universes, reimagining them as having always existed within the same universe.

Considering the complicating repercussions of retcons and multiverses, one might imagine that a retcon that knitted together a multiverse into one might be a simple solution to superhero franchises' continuity woes. After all, *Crisis on Infinite Earths* provided a fresh start as a hard retcon while also effectively erasing the need to remember multiversal counterparts that are no longer canonical. However, this was decidedly not the case. While the new DC Universe was nominally a restart, "creators had to pick and choose from prior continuity" (Friedenthal 88) rather than build from scratch; once this began, the vast differences between character storylines once again became difficult to reconcile with one another. In the years since *Crisis on Infinite Earths*, the DC Universe has undergone multiple retcons, and the DC Multiverse has returned as a standard feature of the company's cosmology; other attempts to revise the multiverse to a more manageable size have had similar results. Even when these strategies are combined to provide a completely fresh start in a singular timeline, the industry's default of telling multiple complex stories simultaneously inevitably requires further use of both retcons and multiverses to carry itself forward. The nature of long-term collaborative storytelling in superhero comics, it seems, is to be forever revising, rebooting, and adding alternatives to existing stories.

Conclusion

Collaborative authorship is a complicated process, especially when it entails successive creative teams with little or no contact with one another, each producing stories according to their own, sometimes conflicting visions. Such large-scale and long-term group productions are bound to generate inconsistencies, exacerbating the industry's need for continual, ever-changing storytelling along with a long history of promising consistent continuity. In terms of helping to reconcile these paradoxical needs, the retcon and the multiverse are vital tools to keep these companies' storyworlds from collapsing under their own massive weight. The retcon allows for revisions of various scales to change our understanding of the past, while the multiverse breathes life into adjacent storyworlds that center hitherto unexplored storytelling possibilities, which can be later incorporated into the "main" universe if desired. Both work to allow for changes to existing franchises while reconciling past continuity, either by changing it, wiping it clean, or suggesting alternative, simultaneously existing timelines. However, as I explained in this chapter, neither of these strategies nor their combined version—the multiversal retcon—is fully capable of creating a continuity that is easily manageable for creators and readers of varying participation levels. It seems that both creators and consumers of superhero comics will forever wrangle with the stop-and-start, ever-branching nature of long-term collaborative storytelling.

CHAPTER 4

SHARING THE SANDBOX
Corporate Interests and Fandoms

Introduction

It is an undisputed fact that mainstream superhero comics is a for-profit industry. Both DC Comics and Marvel Comics produce hundreds of pages depicting the companies' character properties not out of the sole desire to tell stories, but to make money. If they could continue printing the same stories ad nauseam and still turn a profit, the two companies likely would. While the creators who work for these publishers may be passionate about the stories they are working on, at a corporate level continuing and expanding on these existing properties are means to a financial end.

This chapter is not about this kind of writing, but the kinds of creation and collaboration that are not produced for monetary gain. It turns to a different understanding of collaborative authorship by examining the types of writing that are not sanctioned by the stories' copyright holders—namely, comics fandom. Through discussion of comic book fandom's unique history as a participatory culture and through exploration of how fans expand and transform official media properties through collective canon and fan creations such as fanfiction, a broader understanding of comic readership and fan participation as acts of cocreatorship that blur the lines between consumer and creator emerges.

"No-Prize": Participation and Comics Fandom

The idea of fans as participants is a relatively recent one. Although the term "fan" has etymological roots in the Latin "faniticus"—referring to temple servants and religious devotees (Jenkins, *Textual Poachers* 12)—the word "fan" in its current usage first appeared in the nineteenth century to refer to followers of professional sports teams and female theatergoers (Jenkins, *Textual Poachers* 12). In both of these cases, the position of the fan is constructed as one of pure spectator, not participant; the sports fans enjoyed watching their favorite teams and reading about their exploits, while the female theater enthusiasts were derisively called "Matinee Girls" by male critics who "claimed [they] had come to admire the actors rather than the plays" (Jenkins, *Textual Poachers* 12).

This idea of fans as purely viewers carried well into the twentieth century with its attendant rise of televised media. Because the television only projects media content and does not allow instantaneous dialogue between creators and viewers, many academics such as John Ellis and Lawrence Grossberg came to believe that televised media creates an "indifferent" media environment that made "the very idea of a television *fan* seem strange," leaving only "a casual and emotionally distanced spectator" (Grossberg 132, emphasis original; Jenkins, *Textual Poachers* 55; see Ellis).

Fan studies, which began its rise in the 1990s, has taken efforts to refute this view of television fans as passive recipients of culture by giving critical attention to grassroots fan communities that arose around various television franchises, particularly science-fiction shows such as *Star Trek*. Indeed, modern-day fans are often best described not by their passive consumption but by their interaction with the canon texts as part of organized social networks (Lopes 93).

Rather than seeing fans as just recipients, fan studies has argued that the activities performed by these fan groups—recording, cataloging, scene analysis, fan writing, etc.—are forms of meaning-making, thereby creating unauthorized and unanticipated forms of participation. Drawing from Roland Barthes's differentiation between readerly texts, which "need only to be interpreted by readers" (Busse 25; see Barthes, "From Work to Text" 161–63), and writerly texts, which "are constructed with every reading process" (Busse 25; see Barthes, "From Work to Text" 161–63), fan studies explains that fans do not just receive television shows as closed texts but "commit the most aggressive form of reading: with their Barthesian way of literally making any text a writerly text, they become writers of that text, scribbling into the margins and taking the characters, worlds, and plots for a spin" (Busse 36). The intense reading, interpretation, and creative response that are associated with modern fandom, fan studies argues, is in and of itself a type of writing in which fandom takes the received text and makes it their own. But despite the rapid growth of fan studies, very little attention has been paid to the role of fandom in superhero comics.

Perhaps because the discipline arose as a refutation of this stereotyping of television viewers as passive consumers, "[t]he majority of fan fiction scholarship deals with film and television fandoms" (Hellekson and Busse, "Fan Fiction as Literature" 20). While there is quite a bit of crossover between film and comics fandom, particularly with the rise of superhero-based blockbuster movies and TV/streaming service shows, the history of fandom in comics is radically different from that of television or film fandoms.

One of the central ideas that studies of television fandom has worked to counteract is the stereotype that television programs are inherently one-way communication: the broadcast is projected into the consumers' living rooms to be absorbed, with no (preinternet) established structure for viewers to interact with the show's creators. In contrast, fan activities are conceived as a way of "talking back" to their culture. Yet even when the active nature of television and film fandom is acknowledged by the public and media companies, it is often disparaged. Henry Jenkins, Karen Hellekson and Kristina Busse, and Francesca Coppa all point to the 1986 *Saturday Night Live* sketch "Trekkies" as a telling example of how the public and content creators treat fan culture (Jenkins, *Textual Poachers* 9–12; Hellekson and Busse, "Fan Communities and Affect" 131; Coppa 220). In the sketch, the week's host, William Shatner, who played Captain James T. Kirk on the show and in the film versions, attends a fan convention that paints *Star Trek* fans (whose collective moniker gives us the sketch's title) in a particularly distasteful light.

All of the attendants, to a man (and they are only men), mill about the convention floor with their shoulders in a seemingly permanent hunch. The majority wear thick-lensed spectacles, and several wear Vulcan-style rubber ears. One even wears a too-tight "I Grok Spock" T-shirt.[1] This is, of course, playing to stereotype, which is not unusual for a late-night comedy sketch. However, it is the behavior of these "Trekkies" that cements this sketch in fandom history. Two attendees admire one of their finds—a copy of a photo of the original cast for a steep price ("only $60")—and then make fun of a third for misremembering Yeoman Rand's cabin number (*Watch Saturday Night Live Highlight*). Finally, the attendees turn their attention to the convention's special guests. As Jenkins summarizes:

When Shatner arrives, he is bombarded with questions from fans who want to know about minor characters in individual episodes (which they cite by both title and sequence number), who seem to know more about his private life than he does, and who demand such trivial information as the combination to Kirk's safe. Finally, in incredulity and frustration, Shatner turns to the crowd: "Get a life, will you people? I mean, I mean, for crying out loud, it's just a TV show!" Shatner urges the fans to move out of their parent's [*sic*] basements and to proceed with adult experiences ("you, there, have you ever kissed a girl?"), to put their fannish interests behind them. The fans look confused at first, then, progressively more hurt and embarrassed. Finally, one desperate fan asks, "Are you saying we should pay more attention to the movies?" Enraged, Shatner storms off the stage, only to be confronted by an equally angry convention organizer. After a shoving match and a forced rereading of his contract, an embarrassed Shatner takes the stage again and tells the much-relieved fans they have just watched a "recreation of the evil Captain Kirk from episode 27, 'The Enemy Within.'" (Jenkins, *Textual Poachers* 9–10; see *Watch Saturday Night Live Highlight*)

Although meant to be comical, "[f]ans saw little comic exaggeration in the *Saturday Night Live* sketch, in any case, since Shatner had repeatedly expressed many of these same sentiments in public interviews"; other contemporary descriptions of television fans, like a *Newsweek* description of a Trekkie convention that appeared two days after "Trekkies," described members of fandom as "'kooks' obsessed with trivia . . . misfits and 'crazies' . . . as childish adults" (Jenkins, *Textual Poachers* 11). A disdainful attitude emanates from these depictions of fans.

However, while such scholars of television fandom take that dynamic as typical for the time period, this was not the case in the interactions between comic book publishers (and the creators who they hired) and comic book fandom. On the contrary, comic books, particularly superhero comics, have a long history of centering dialogue between fans and creators, which has placed comic book fandom in a unique position regarding its relationship with the object of their enthusiasm.

Comic book fandom took a long time to grow into the form we recognize today. As Ted White notes, "Comics fandom took a long time to develop and did so in fits and starts. . . . By 1960, comics had been around for over 25 years, but comics fandom was still in its infancy" (White 99; qtd. in Woo 116). That said, early comic book publishers actively encouraged fan participation and later the creation of fan communities through the inclusion of a letters section in comic books. Early comic book publishers maintained "the tradition of science fiction magazines from the 1930s" ("Letter Columns [Concept]"), from which superhero comics began as an offshoot,[2] by publishing readers' letters within their comics in the form of a letters column, "borrowing from the idea behind letters to the editor at newspapers" ("Letter Columns [Concept]"). The letters column first appeared in a comic book with DC's non-superhero *Real Fact Comics* #3 in 1946 ("Real Fact Comics #3 [DC, 1946] Condition"), but the innovation quickly became routine practice in DC's superhero comics following *Superman* #124's first use of a letter column page in 1958 (Gordon 120). Marvel, which was formed decades after DC, began including letter columns, complete with Stan Lee's own "Stan's Soapbox" essays, following the massive amount of fan mail the company received in response to *Fantastic Four* #1 (Lee, David et al.).[3] These letter sections—often given headers that played on the series title, like *The Flash*'s "Speed Reading" or the X-Men's "X-pressions"— became a part of comic book tradition.

While superhero comics are now a major presence in the mass-media environment, it is important to remember that until relatively recently they were considered niche media. Before the appearance of the letters section in comics, former DC editor Dennis "Denny" O'Neil notes, "there was no arena [for fans] to exchange opinions" (Pearson and Uricchio 23). Reading comic books before the incorporation of a letters column would seem much as Ellis and Grossberg later viewed television watching: an isolating experience in which consumers were cut off from communicating with others regarding the media they are consuming.

The printing of fan letters within the official publication along with the custom of the issue's writer(s) and artist(s) responding to these fans, however, altered this dynamic. A letters section like those featured in comic books elevates the position of the comic book fan and their reactions to the original work. While television and film fans can write letters to their favorite showrunners and directors, their opinions will never be incorporated into the work that inspired their writing. In superhero comics, on the other hand, fan responses are routinely incorporated into the series' following issues. Because of this, these fan letters are placed alongside later installments of the story they are commenting on; in other words, the publishers of superhero comics effectively transform fan commentary into officially produced—though delayed—paratext. As the printed letters are nominally representative of the overall variety of submissions (though sometimes with grammatical corrections and with the publishers as the ultimate curators [Pearson and Uricchio 29, Stein 51]), these publishers are allowing a space in which fans express a variety of opinions within a sanctioned space. Additionally, creators are expected to respond to said commentary, ensuring a dialogue between mass-media creators and consumers about the work in progress that promoted "heightened degrees of authorial engagement *and* reader involvement" (Stein 39, emphasis original). These sections acted as avenues in which fans could not only express a variety of opinions regarding the work but have a reasonable expectation of two-way communication with the creators of their favored works. Thus, the letters section became an officially produced, built-in space to publicly share opinions about media content not only with other fans but with the creators of said media incorporated into the text itself—an opportunity unavailable to most film and television fans, even with the rise of Web 2.0.

Not only did superhero comics provide space for fan letters to be published as paratextual commentary, but the industry also explicitly provided incentive for these fans to take a detail-oriented and at times critical approach to the stories. Beginning in the 1960s, partly in response to the attention *Fantastic Four* #1 received, superhero comics began to shift their demographic attention away from children to adolescents and college-aged adults. This shift to older readers, combined with the rise of greater continuity in comic books,[4] led to much more complicated storytelling: "Whereas most earlier stories had been short and self-contained, returning the narrative to status quo in a few pages," Benjamin Woo notes, "readers now had to keep track of what had happened in previous issues and other series" (117). While comic book companies took special care to keep track of the continuity of their own properties, such a multipronged narrative exercise was bound to generate errors. These older, more dedicated fans often noticed these mistakes, notifying creators of these inconsistencies via fan letter. Rather than brush off these criticisms, many companies publishing superhero comics chose to encourage their fan base by rewarding such careful reading. More established companies such as National Comics (later DC Comics) offered these fans various prizes such as cash awards or free issues. Marvel Comics, then much less wealthy than many of its competitors, did not have the budget to send awards to fans (Lee, David et al.) and thus did not offer these traditional rewards. Instead, Marvel offered what would become the most widely remembered of these reader rewards: astute Marvel letter-writers received a fancy but empty envelope that congratulated the reader for receiving a "Marvel No-Prize."[5] These envelopes are collector's items even today, decades after Marvel ended this practice.[6]

Though originally used as promotional prizes to reward repeat and thorough consumers and since abandoned, these prizes were also influential in the shaping of comic book fandom. While television and film franchises often have an uneasy relationship with fans who dissect their creations down to its most minute details, superhero comics historically welcomed treating their properties as writerly texts, even offering tangible rewards. By giving out prizes, comic book companies provided physical—and in the case of cash prizes or free issues, financial—incentives to avid, meticulous readers, who pounced on any suggestions of continuity errors, leading comic book fandom to develop into what Kristina Busse calls "possibly the most comprehensive and complex of fandoms" (Busse 103). While William Shatner and the writers of *Saturday Night Live* derided Trekkies for having an encyclopedic knowledge of *Star Trek*'s minutia and for pursuing further details to memorize, comic book companies actively encouraged such knowledge and behavior, effectively creating a fan base that is intimately connected with and engaging in a dialogue with its creators.

This dialogue, however, is not just between individual fans and comic book creators, but a community of likeminded (or at least like-interested) fans engaging with each other. The mainstream companies had a hand in the creation of these exchanges by acting "as mediators of genre evolution by enabling readers to refine their critical skills and by fostering public controversy" (Stein 36). In addition to incentivizing their fan base to become involved and detail-oriented in their reading and commenting practices, the use of the letters section as paratextual dialogue also played a transformational role in the development of comics fandom as a community. While the first letters columns in comics were originally geared towards featuring and responding to the questions of young readers, the comments in the section grew in complexity as the genre began to attract older readers in the 1960s. As letter-writing fans became accustomed to having a letters space, fan writers also started becoming more comfortable with the authorial capabilities such a paratextual space enabled (Stein 63). Fan letters, on average, became longer and more detailed ("Letter Columns [Concept]"). Additionally, fans were likely to write frequently; of his sampling of 2,034 fan letters from 1958 to 1978, Ian Gordon found "8 percent of writers wrote 25 percent of the letters. The average number of letters published from this group of writers who had two or more letters published was almost four letters" (127).

Among these letter-writers, several earned reputations through their frequent appearances in letters sections. DC fan Peter Sanderson, for example, is still known today for his "lengthy, well-reasoned, and impressively erudite missives [which] forced [DC Comics] editor [Julius aka "Julie"] Schwartz to expand the lettercols [aka letters column section] in his classic, mid-sixties Silver Age books to a second, separate page (such as 'Flash-Grams—Extra,' 'Letters To the Batcave—Extra,' and 'JLA Mailroom—Special Peter Sanderson Edition') to facilitate Peter's sharp analysis" (Hembeck).

Still, despite the considerable thought and attention these letter-writers gave to their correspondence, they were primarily communicating to the publishing company and the series' creative talent, leaving fans largely disconnected with one another. But superhero comics used the letters section as a means of cultivating the comics fandom into a community when Julius Schwartz "began publishing the letter writers' complete addresses with 1961's [The] Brave and the Bold #35, for which he had solicited letters of comment from 'some of his better correspondents'" (Woo 117; see Fox and Kubert). While the implementation of a fan letters section had previously allowed fans to have their opinions printed and responded to by series creators, Woo sees this further innovation as a catalyst for the formation of comics fandom communities: "By providing evidence of others' responses to the comics and enabling fans to connect with one another, the letters pages helped knit readers together as a kind of community. Some took the further step of creating fan clubs, such as the EC Fan-Addict Club and the Merry Marvel Marching Society" (117).

Although most of the fan clubs described by early fan studies were organized through grassroots channels without control or permission of media companies, these comic fan clubs were often actively promoted by the comic book companies. An archived 1972 letter to Stan Lee reveals that then-Marvel editor Sol Brodsky had begun making arrangements with the Hallmark Minting Service to create collectible "coin-medallions" to give, along with other items, to members of the latest official Marvel fan club, the Friends of Ol' Marvel, aka FOOM (Walerstein). In this typewritten letter, Mike Walerstein of Hallmark Minting Service explicitly suggests using the coins as a means of rewarding and encouraging membership:

> Lets [sic] send an insert along with [the coin-medallion] offering the following: FOOM MEMBERS . . . . .ARE :THE FIRST TO BE OFFERED THIS FIRST IN A SERIES OF THE GREATEST HERO'S IN THE WORLD . . . . FOOM MEMBERS

WILL GET THE LOWEST NUMBERS ON THE COINS AND OF
COURSE THIS WILL MAKE THEM OF GREATER VALUE . . .
. . . . JUST ONE OF THE MANY ADVANTAGES OF BEING A
FOOM MEMBER . . . . THE
GENERAL PUBLIC WILL HAVE TO WAIT. (Walerstein, spelling
and punctuation original. The last two instances of "Foom" are both
typed in red ink.)

In a handwritten note on the letter, Lee suggests advertising the
club using a full-page advertisement within Marvel comics themselves, thereby giving official promotion and incentive to join fan
communities. While decades later Henry Jenkins and other early
fan scholars described the creators of televised shows like *Star Trek*
as markedly separate from its early fan bases—Shatner yelling at
Trekkies to "get a life!"—corporate copyright holders and creators of
superhero comics not only provided space for fans to interact with
them but played an active role in promoting the creation of focused
fan communities through rewarding both the hunting down and
cataloguing of contradictory minutiae and the joining of nascent fan
communities. While preinternet television fans may have operated
separately from the people who produced the subject of interest,
and may have even faced their public derision, comics fandom was
and still is propped up by comic book publishers. The lines between
corporate and fan cultures are particularly blurred in the case of
superhero comics fandom.

That said, this does not mean that the relationship between comic
book companies and fans is necessarily a comfortable one. Although
comic book companies as an industry historically cultivated the
growth of their attendant fandom, fans do not always act in ways
that these companies desire. On the contrary, while comic book fans
supply a steady stream of cash for comic book publishers, they are
also a source of contention for copyright holders, especially in the
areas of emotional ownership, the rise of transformative fanworks,
and the ever-blurring line between creator and consumer.

Sandbox Wars: Who "Owns" Superheroes?

Given the history outlined above of early comics fandom, it is perhaps unsurprising that fans reacted to decades of comic book companies' active encouragement of fan involvement in the form of letter columns, fan awards, and the cultivation of early fan communities by becoming a highly participatory fan culture. Readers of superhero comics tend to be deeply involved—both financially and often emotionally—in the characters and stories to the extent that comics fan communities feel a sense of ownership over these properties. This can cause a number of problems for comic book companies, which now face an uneasy relationship with the very fans upon whose consumption they rely.

The crux of this tension can perhaps best be understood through an extension of superhero comics industry's metaphor of the sandbox. When describing the comic book industry, the idea of the sandbox is repeatedly used to describe the relationship individual creators have to a company's fictional universe:[7] they have been granted temporary permission to play with that company's play area and with its toys—that is, the company's universe and a limited number of characters—but they are expected to leave DC or Marvel's toys largely as they found them and can have the right to play with them revoked at any moment.[8] This metaphor has become a common way to discuss the narrative universe and the ability of various creators to work inside of it.

To take this idea further, comic book companies had originally paid for the creation of the sandbox by employing its original creators; as corporate copyright owners, Marvel and DC are the legal owners of their own proprietary sandboxes. Because these sandboxes are officially theirs, and they can hire or fire creators sanctioned to use their space and toys, these companies feel that they are in full control of it and can make any creative decisions they choose, making up stories, evolving characters, and changing their narrative universes to fit whatever mood takes them while they play with their properties.

Comic book readers do not have official permission to play with these companies' toys; instead, purchasing and reading comics allow them to be seated outside of the sandbox and watch the play that occurs within it. But rather than just treating these readers as passive observers to their narrative play, for decades comic book publishers have invited them to offer input on the events that occur within the sandbox. For more than half a century, comic book publishers have set aside pages, which could be filled with more advertisements or extended story, to feature letter column sections—in effect pausing the creators' play in the sandbox for them to interact with their audiences and for the spectators to give direct commentary and feedback—and gave various prizes to those who made particularly insightful, detail-oriented, or otherwise noteworthy contributions. In a few notable instances, the sandbox owners have even given fans the ability to directly influence the future of the sandbox, including the (in)famous 1988 Batman *A Death in the Family* story arc, when DC Comics, inspired by *Saturday Night Live*'s 1982 Larry the Lobster publicity stunt (Weldon 147–48), allowed readers to decide whether Jason Todd—alias the second Robin—lived or died (Pearson and Uricchio 21).

Although comic book readers are not officially allowed within the sandbox, decades of copyright holders eliciting (and sometimes heeding) their readers' feedback has led these fans to develop a collective sense of expectations regarding activities that should take place there. For example, because superhero comics long rewarded readers that recognized discrepancies or "errors" in continuity, the genre's dedicated fans have collectively cultivated an eye for detail and an expectation for such consistency. Ironically, this strong demand for seamless continuity eventually led to the end of the Marvel's No-Prize. One of the greatest advocates for the Marvel No-Prize in the 1980s was Marvel editor Mark Gruenwald, who reportedly gave the award not only to fans who pointed out continuity errors but also to those who came up with clever explanations for canonical events. However, in a multipart 1986 letter in *The*

West Coast Avengers #10 and *The Avengers* #269, Gruenwald said he was ending the award because it rewarded nitpicking instead of attention to the story (Gruenwald, "Mark's Remarks"; Gruenwald, "Mark's Remarks").

However, just because the No-Prize and similar reader prizes have fallen away does not mean that readers no longer partake in the engagement practices that were nurtured by these rewards. While neither Marvel nor DC continue to offer rewards for pointing out continuity errors, comics fandom has collectively been trained to notice and prioritize such details, and any such changes are bound to attract the notice of comic book fans.

This can be particularly troublesome in the age of the internet. The internet, particularly social media, has made comic book fandom more accessible, allowing "marginal fans [to find] a new social space to intervene in comic book culture" (Lopes 172–73). This can be positive and negative. While this means more people are able to engage with enthusiasts and may be drawn into the fold, this ease of access means that rather than writing any criticisms to comic book companies and then waiting and hoping to be chosen for publications, fans can now quickly and publicly criticize any creative decisions they feel violate a story's narrative premise, find others who share their feelings (positive or negative) about a particular narrative or artistic decision, or simply "@" the creators involved in an attempt to get their immediate and direct attention.

This internet activity is critical when considering current comic book fan communities and its relationship with comic book publishers. While the letters pages at the end of comic books were (and still are) sites in which fans can participate in paratextual exchange within the text itself—and, if published, in more direct conversation with the official creators (Gordon 118)—they are also limited by page length and are moderated by the companies that publish and respond to only a select few submissions. The internet, on the other hand, has a virtually unlimited amount of space for curious and passionate comic book readers to interact with each other on social media pages, chats, forums, and more. In these online spaces, fans may engage in conversation with the publishing companies and the professional creators who created the comic books they read, but they can also directly engage with each other with a speed and frequency that would be difficult to impossible to replicate offline. These communities, through the practices of fandom itself, may choose to work with an altogether different set of unofficial rules and expectations. These practices can be seen as an unsanctioned form of collaborative authorship—one that has profound effects on how these communities perceive and engage with the official texts.

The Formation of the Fanon

When describing how *Star Trek* fans in the 1980s treated recordings of their favorite show, Jenkins observes that fans "often blur the boundaries between aesthetic judgement and textual interpretation" (Jenkins, *Textual Poachers* 98). While these fans would consume the text wholesale—often memorizing select scenes—they would often pore over and discuss the slightest details and their implications, a level of analysis that is often the subject to conventions similar (though "less rigidly defined or precisely followed" [Jenkins, *Textual Poachers* 89]) to those followed within the academy.[9] Comic book fans are no different; just as Jenkins's *Star Trek* fans avidly discussed recordings of episodes, every week comic book fans dissect and interpret each new installment depicting their favorite characters, sometimes down to the expressions in individual panels.

Within comic book fandom, there are two major trends in how fans proceed with such dissection and interpretation. The first is perhaps the most straightforward: by reading and sharing individual takeaways with others with similar interests. For the same reasons that people join book clubs or discuss their favorite movies or TV shows with others, fans of superhero comics can find deep engagement in the text as a community, plumbing its depths as a writerly text (rather than the readerly text as it may have been intended) in order to gain both deeper meaning and camaraderie within the community.

These discussions—whether online or offline—serves two functions for comic book fans and creators. The first is that these discussions nurture collective fandom memory. As discussed in the previous chapter, the sheer vastness of history within superhero comics—its many twists, turns, and complete reversals—can be referenced, elaborated on, or negated at any time. When fans of superhero comics discuss what is currently or previously canon or any tidbits of industry history, they are interpolating these pieces of canon to revive and invigorate collective memory of what is and what has been, fostering collective memory of this genre's long, complicated history.

But these fans do more than just exchange knowledge. By collectively discussing the current canon in relation to what came before, these fans collectively create a common understanding of the fictional properties they are examining. Although characters and storyworlds can change drastically over time—and even from creative team to creative team—these readers enjoy picking apart, cataloguing, and discussing these differences. But while they are doing so, they are also collectively deciding what plotlines or details are important parts to remember and that are key parts of the canon, and which ones are less relevant to understanding the character and storyworld. Over time, these fans have a solidified understanding of the characters that may be completely different from what the publishing companies' current editorial goals may wish, because these fans are as much invested in the creative analysis of their fellow readers as much as—if not more so—than the canon text itself.

However, in the face of such detailed examination, the limitations of the officially published material that drives many of these conversations between fans can soon become evident. Some of these limitations are due to problems in the storytelling itself. Contradictions—some obviously retcons, some more likely to be mistakes—will inevitably appear within serially produced media.

Certain narrative decisions, in the rush to finish in accordance with deadlines, will sometimes be underexplored or not properly explained within the canon material.

Other limitations that these fans perceive, on the other hand, are due to limitations in how the industry conceives of itself. As a genre whose creators and publishers historically saw themselves as appealing to mostly straight male readers, superhero comics still often focus on action and themes that publishers feel will appeal to that particular demographic to the exclusion of other types of storytelling. However, this idea of superhero comics having a mostly male fandom is impossible to determine with accurate reader statistics. Comic book companies typically only count the number of issues sold, even when readers often buy multiple issues at once (Parsons 67); when they do try to collect demographic information, it is often regarding the readership of a particular property and becomes closely guarded proprietary data (Woo 115). Even the publishers of these comic books may not know with certainty that their own conceptions regarding their genre's audience are accurate. Bias in the perceived gender of their readership affects the stories that are told, and how they are told.

Since superhero comics, as an industry, historically saw (and in many cases still sees) itself as catering mostly to "boys and young men" (Morrison 40), it tends to focus on story elements thought to appeal to this demographic; that is, more pages are spent on fight scenes with the supervillain of the week than other aspects of these characters' lives, such as lengthy portrayals of dates with their romantic partners. Even when female readers are not actively antagonized through "gratuitously offensive characterization of women" (Salkowitz 78–79) in comic books,[10] story elements that are traditionally associated with them are kept to the margins.

But fans—particularly those in groups less commonly catered to, such as women[11]—have a long history of interacting with media that was not created with them in mind. In response, Jenkins notes, these underprivileged or ignored media consumers tend to adapt their approach to media and "radically reconceptualize" these stories to accommodate their interests (Jenkins, *Textual Poachers* 114). In particular, these people shift their attention to the margins of the text, "imagining the characters as having a life existing apart from the fictional narrative" (Jenkins, *Textual Poachers* 114). When faced with the text's narrative gaps—i.e., the parts of a person's life that would not appear in a superhero comic—these fans do not satisfy themselves with the fact that some aspects of these characters' existences are merely unstated. Instead, they use their overarching understanding of these characters and their general narrative universe gained from multiple, focused readings/viewings of the text and fan analysis—what Jenkins refers to the "meta-text" (Jenkins, *Textual Poachers* 98, 101)—to "offe[r] speculations and extrapolations" or speculative interpretations to fill these narrative gaps (Jenkins, *Textual Poachers* 101).

These personal, creative interpretations are referred to by fans as "headcanons"—because they come from their brains, not from the canon texts—and can vary in scope. A headcanon can range from theorizations about a character's preferred workout playlist to attempts "to better explain the motivation and context of narrative events" (Jenkins, *Textual Poachers* 101) and everything in between. However, whether a headcanon is trivially small or wide-ranging in scope, it represents a fundamental change in how these fans think about and approach the original text as much as it represents a fundamental change for how these fans conceptualize the relative positions of creator and consumer.

No matter what the headcanon's ultimate implications, its creation requires two vital components: an understanding of a metatext and "emotional realism." Jenkins defines emotional realism as "an interpretive fiction fans construct in the process of making meaning of popular narratives" (Jenkins, *Textual Poachers* 107) that posits a consistency of rules and underlying ideologies that define "[w]hat counts as 'plausible'" (Jenkins, *Textual Poachers* 107). In other words, regardless of whether the story is set in our reality or depicts flying aliens with super-strength, there should be a similar emotional logic that both allows readers to emotionally engage with the text and "allows fans to draw upon their own personal backgrounds as one means of extrapolating beyond the information explicitly found within the aired episodes" (Jenkins, *Textual Poachers* 107).

Take, for example, a simple headcanon about Superman. Basically every adult in the English-speaking world (and many beyond it) has at least some understanding of this character and his backstory, even if they have never actually read a Superman comic book. But, to my knowledge, the character has never been said to have a favorite ice cream flavor in any materials produced by DC Comics. If, like these fans who create headcanons, we were to imagine Superman as a person who exists outside of his fictional narrative, what would we decide his favorite flavor to be?

One could say that, since Superman in a flying, super-strong alien with heat vision, all logical "rules" we could apply to such questions do not work and that one could answer with any random flavor, or one could simply say it's whatever DC Comics and the creators it employs decide. In a purely objective sense, these are the most correct answers. But fans who are creating headcanons using the premise of emotional realism would for the most part not accept such conclusions as the final answer and would instead make a number of possible suggestions and argue for these headcanons using canonical evidence, metatextual schema, and their own emotional experiences. These fans of Superman would likely turn to his canonical backstory—he is the last son of the planet Krypton who was raised from infancy or early childhood by Martha "Ma" and Jonathan "Pa" Kent on their farm in Smallville, Kansas, before moving to Metropolis to become a reporter and superhero—as a basis of understanding his upbringing and to gain a broad understanding of his possible tastes and values. Furthermore, such a fan could point to what is already stated within the text about his culinary tastes, particularly the numerous instances in which Clark/Superman expresses love for Ma Kent's homemade pies. This love of his mother's cooking fits a metatextual understanding of Superman as an embodiment of Clark's down-home, middle-American upbringing and subsequent values—an association that has given him the nickname "the big blue Boy Scout" both inside and outside his fictional universe. Taken together, evidence from the canon material and metatextual knowledge could lead these fans to conclude that Superman's preferences for ice cream would—like his love of his mother's pies—reflect a down-to-earth upbringing and evoke traditional values and tastes.

At this point, developing a headcanon becomes less an analysis of text—or even of metatext—and more a maintenance of emotional consistency. What flavor "fits" this canonical and metatextual idea of the Man of Steel that exists only in a fan's imagination? What has a sense of emotional realism for them?

It could easily be argued that such arguments point to a variety of flavors—maybe vanilla or chocolate chip ice cream, or some barely concealed reference to Superman ice cream (perhaps by another name),[12] or some Kent family secret recipe. Perhaps, as you read the preceding paragraph, you came to one of these conclusions or another altogether—your own personal headcanon. To me, the answer is butter pecan. As stated before, there is no logical reason for this answer; there is no textual evidence to cite to support why I believe that this would be the case. But based on my own personal experiences and sense of emotional realism, the idea of the Last Son of Krypton with a bowl of butter pecan ice cream—simple but comforting, reminiscent of both Ma Kent's baking and my own childhood memories of my mother cracking the thousands of pecans that fell into our yard from our neighbor's tree—*feels* right. It is more in keeping with my metatextual understanding of his character than any other flavor. The idea that this would be the Man of Tomorrow's favorite flavor is intrinsically tied to my understanding of this character; it reflects the canon that lives only inside my head.

As is evident in this short example, headcanons can confound stereotypes regarding the consumption of mass media in a number of ways. First, the practice of creating headcanons transforms a fan's relationship with the media they consume. While Barthes may have seen readers who must make their own meaning from writerly texts as "no longer a consumer, but a producer of the text" (Barthes, *S/Z: An Essay* 4; qtd. in Busse 107) in terms of making meaning, fans who create headcanons are literally producing elements of the storyworld that are not included in the source text. They are, in other words, writing. Although headcanons are a product derived from both the canonical material and the fan's own imagination—their head, not the canon—they are nonetheless attempts to expand the canon, of fans taking themselves out of the role of passive consumer and instead inhabiting the role of creator.

This expansion of the canon also blurs the line between strict textual interpretation, personal experience, and aesthetic preferences. Although it took me almost pages to explain the formation of one particular headcanon, these speculative interpretations often happen instantaneously. This blurring can affect how fans approach the source text. A fan's metatext, as a "composite view" of multiple interactions with the source text (Jenkins, *Textual Poachers* 107), can be affected and colored by what that fan reads regardless of its canonicity, as long as it does not conflict with their current metatext. Therefore, other fans' shared headcanons can also affect how these readers approach their source text, including how they "comprehend and evaluate the character's conduct in particular narrative situations" (Jenkins, *Textual Poachers* 107). While headcanons may originally be derived in response to gaps within the canon, they also inevitably affect how subsequent canonical materials are received.

That said, it is important to note that part of what creates variations in headcanons is not only natural variances in personal opinion but variances in reading practices. When reading a text, Busse observes, readers themselves naturally alter it:

> As readers engage with a text, they produce a personal and idiosyncratic reading of their canon that then becomes the basis for their interpretation and writing. This may be as minimal as focusing on

one character and his or her interaction at the expense of others, or as major as excluding entire seasons after a central event (such as replacement of an actor or death of a beloved character). Identifying with one character while ignoring another, or foregrounding one scene while neglecting another produces a highly idiosyncratic reading. . . . Fans often regard their recollections as canon, when in fact every reading already includes a variety of interpretations beyond the base facts. (Busse 108)

Even when interacting with the same source material, then, Busse suggests that idiosyncrasies of memory, attention, and interest create different metatextual understandings. These differences are multiplied in the context of superhero comics fandom. Over the course of their histories, DC Comics and Marvel Comics have published immense amounts of material; anthologies dedicated to especially popular characters can take up multiple volumes that are hundreds of pages each. In contrast to film and television fandoms, in which "it is important to see *all* the episodes 'in order'" (Jenkins, *Textual Poachers* 99, emphasis original), such an expectation for comics fandom would require unlimited amounts of money and time. Such a task is, practically speaking, impossible. Thus, the metatextual understandings of comics fans, and many resulting headcanons, can highly conflict with one another.

These differences in fans' metatexts and headcanons, as well as the ways in which headcanons work to expand and modify existing canon, is particularly evident in fan-created fictional works otherwise known as fan fiction.[13] If headcanons can be viewed as fans "scribbling into the margins" (Busse 36), then fan fiction occurs when these fans "tak[e] the characters, worlds, and plots for a spin" (Busse 36) by using their favorite media and its canon as building blocks to construct their own stories. In fan fiction, fans take control of these storyworlds for themselves—taking positions as writers in addition to their previous statuses as consumers and commenters.

In fan creations—videos, art, but particularly fan-created fiction—headcanons and their effects on the source canon are given life in several ways. For example, by revisiting key scenes within the canonical text—often multiple times—fanfiction writers "negotiate multiple interpretations of characters, dynamics, and events, [and] often fill in scenes or thoughts that are absent in the source text" (Busse 58; see also Jenkins, *Textual Poachers* 162). Similarly, fan fiction creators can change the metatextual viewpoint through which the canonical material is viewed, either by shifting attention to refocus on side-characters, "invert[ing] or question[ing] the moral universe of the primary text" (Jenkins, *Textual Poachers* 168), or even shifting the source text's genre (e.g., from action to romance [see Jenkins, *Textual Poachers* 162–77]). These viewpoint shifts interrogate the text by suggesting that the perspective of non-protagonists are worth exploring and asking what the canonical storyworld would be for someone who was not a point-of-view character.

But fanfiction can also go much further in transforming the source text. Unlike the original work's creator(s), fan creators are "unrestricted by commercial impetus" (Busse 58); there is no need to worry about disrupting the status quo to the point of turning away money-paying readers. Because of this, fan imaginations tend to run wild in their transformative works, and even fundamental aspects of a storyworld are open to interpretation. Genderswap fanfics, for example, are a common fanfiction trope which interrogates the role of gender in the canonical text by changing the gender of one or more characters (typically "swapping" it across the gender binary); meanwhile, other alternate universes (often abbreviated by fanwork creators and readers as "AUs") depict "characters [that] are removed from their original situations and given alternative names and identities" (Jenkins, *Textual Poachers* 171) within a new constructed universe—for example, as college students, coffee shop employees, or mermaids, to name a few popular AU tropes.

No matter the approach of any particular work, these fan works are taking part in a communal conversation regarding the source text. Each time a fanfiction is shared, it is not only engaging in a dialogue with the canonical material but with other fan works; as "[n]o story exists in a vacuum, and very few stories are written with only an awareness of the source and no other interpretations or conversations . . . online fan works respond to, comment on, mimic, or criticize fannish conventions and other texts" (Busse 114).[14] Over time, this discourse can develop its own norms. Subfandoms commonly form around certain fanfic tropes, AUs, or romantic pairings, and certain fan fictions with "a particularly memorable characterization or an especially convincing development of a specific pairing" can earn the status of becoming "required reading" for such fan communities (Busse 113).

Throughout this exchange, a type of unofficial consensus regarding the interpretation of the source texts can begin to form. Interesting and/or convincing portrayals of frequently revisited scenes become popular and repeated through later fanworks, and especially compelling creative headcanons are utilized by other fan authors as inspiration for new stories. Even AUs, which place characters outside of their normal storyworlds, influence fan interpretations by interrogating which aspects of a character—their background, their personality, etc.—could stay constant if they existed outside of their normal narrative environment. To put it another way, these AUs help reveal which character traits are essential to a fan's metatextual understanding of them. Eventually, these interpretations of characters and their storyworlds can become foundational assumptions that fans bring to all versions of the text, fan-created or not. These community-wide headcanons are, appropriately, called "fanon": aspects of the story that do not come from official sources but are nonetheless accepted as canon by large portions of the fandom.

These two groups of superhero comics fans—the ones cataloguing and factually analyzing, and the ones creating headcanons, fanons, and fan works—are engaging in very different activities, and often in very different spaces. However, both groups' means of interacting with and about their chosen texts are doing something fundamentally interesting: they are going beyond what the publishing companies and professional creators have provided them to create new meaning and writing. They aren't passively consuming this content. Instead, they are actively building upon the canon and each other's ideas in a way that continuously elaborates and speculates—on what it was, on what it could have been, on what it is now, on what it possibly could be. In other words, they are writing collaboratively with the source text and officially sanctioned creators as well as with themselves, creating a seemingly endless fount of new writing: analyses, metatextual understandings/fanons, headcanons, and more.

However, this type of collaborative creation that builds on top of itself can create a problem when these fans step away from their fan analyses, fan works, headcanons, and fanon and return to officially produced materials. While fan analysts and fanfic writers are in conversation with "not just the source text and what they themselves bring to it via their personal interpretations but against a vast corpus of other fan fiction" (Busse 113), the creators of canon text are only beholden to the canon's own rules, not those established within the fanon. But although the stories distributed by the mainstream publishers are not affected by the fanon, their readers' perceptions of the characters and what they do may be—sometimes even dramatically so. When the official source violates the expectations set by fanon, they run the risk of these fans (i.e., the ones that are the most engaged with their creations) protesting that the characters are acting "out of character" or "OOC." In other words, the canon material in question is too much in conflict with their own metatexts and headcanons to be properly assimilated. As Daniel Stein observes, "it is neither the creators nor the readers or even the comics themselves the directly bring a certain character, storyline, or series into existence, but indeed the complex interaction of all of these and many other actors whose serial agencies come together in the act of superhero storytelling" (12). While the publishing companies may hold the legal rights to these characters, they are no longer the only ones who control how these characters and stories are received; instead, the perceptions and reactions of fans have a strong impact on how both officially and unofficially created works are perceived by the wider public.

A recent, large-scale example of this within comics fandom can be found in the response to Zack Snyder's 2016 film *Batman v Superman: Dawn of Justice*, which was produced under DC Comic's parent company, Warner Bros. Many fans of Batman criticized Snyder's depiction of the Dark Knight for, among other things, using firearms, claiming that this went against Batman canon. But this is not factually the case: Batman did, in fact, use firearms occasionally in his early comic book appearances, with the character only becoming gun-free afterwards (Daniels, *DC Comics: A Celebration of the World's Favorite Comic Book Heroes* 34; Weldon 13–14). Snyder's depiction of a gun-firing Batman, therefore, was technically in line with older canonical versions of the character. In fact, Snyder's film went against most fans' Batman metatext, in which he avoids using guns.[15] Although DC Comics and Warner Bros. are allowed to do whatever they please with the property, and Batman has been depicted as using guns in the past, the work done by fans as unofficial cowriters via headcanons, fanfiction, and fanon has expanded and transformed the perception of the character in the eyes of the general public, causing Synder's gun-toting Bruce Wayne to become unacceptable to large swathes of the public.

Producer/Consumer: The Blurring Boundaries of Convergent Media

As the above example suggests, mass-media companies can have complicated relationships with the fandoms that form around their creations. This is especially true in the increasingly digital media environment, which Jenkins argues has created a culture of media convergence "where old and new media collide, where grassroots and corporate media intersect, where the power of the media producer and the power of the media consumer interact in unpredictable ways" (Jenkins, *Convergence Culture* 2). Due to the rise of convergence culture, the boundaries between media producers and media consumers have shifted, creating a new normal that must now be negotiated.

First and foremost, the perception and treatment of fans has dramatically changed with the rise of internet-based fandom. While earlier perceptions of mass-media fandoms were that these consumers were childish and needed to "get a life!," the increasingly multimedia distribution of media has required "media companies to rethink old assumptions about what it means to consume media" (Jenkins, *Convergence Culture* 18). This includes how these companies relate to their audience and fandom. In stark contrast to the 1970s and 1980s, when companies such as LucasFilm threatened legal action against fanzines that included pornographic fanfiction (Busse 103; Jenkins, *Textual Poachers* 31), media companies no longer treat fanworks as direct threats to their properties. On the contrary, Busse notes that there are numerous benefits to media companies that encourage fannish behavior in their consumers, including "viewer loyalty, free advertisement, and increased purchase of connected products. Moreover, fans contribute their free labor to add value to sites" through the production of fanworks (Busse 181).

However, this does not mean that corporate media wholeheartedly accepts fandom. Although a certain level of fan enthusiasm is a free and energetic source of viral advertising, "[t]he relationship between fan and producer . . . is not always a happy or comfortable one and is often charged with mutual suspicion, if not open conflict" (Jenkins, *Textual Poachers* 45). While much of fandom's creative productions celebrate a source text—and to a certain extent its creators—creators of transformative works like fanfiction are more likely to criticize the source text than the everyday consumer. Fan fiction, after all, is the product of fans who were not completely satisfied with the source text, and the detail-oriented nature of fan analysis leads these fans to find flaws in the original that the everyday person might simply overlook or ignore. Therefore, while media companies are beginning to cultivate certain aspects of fannish behavior in the manner that comic book companies once did, they are reticent to embrace fandom in its full capacity.

One aspect of full-fledged fandom that appears particularly troubling for these companies appears to be fanfiction. While other types of fan creations—fanart, fanvids, etc.—often entail some level of transformation and interpretation, with fanfiction consumers most directly take the means of storytelling into their own hands. This can cause uneasiness among corporate copyright holders. While they still legally own the properties being transformed, the existence of fanfiction troubles their ability to control the use and reception of their properties. It is no coincidence that Jenkins originally described participatory fans who created fanworks as "textual poachers"—these fans are, in the eyes of corporate producers, taking off with their property for their own, unsanctioned purposes. Even today, when fanfiction writers are no longer under the threat of copyright-infringement lawsuits, creators of these works still challenge given wisdom regarding authorship and creative control (Busse 104). When consumers are just as capable of influencing the interpretation of the original source on a large scale—of creating new material, expanding upon existing properties, and otherwise altering the canon through fan production—the official creators are no longer the sole producers of their creations. Instead, their roles are more akin to cocreators with innumerable unpaid cowriters.

But superhero comics in particular present another factor affecting the industry's relationship to its fandom. As Francesca Coppa observes, even if fans wanted to work in television and film, "the odds of writing a show you like, as opposed to one you're assigned to, are small" (Coppa 220). The production lives of works in this medium are relatively short; film franchises and television shows that have lasted for decades are notable for their rarity. Therefore, when it comes to these properties, the possibility of transitioning from fan to professional contributor—or, in Andrew J. Friedenthal's terms, becoming a "fan-turned-pro" (33)—is almost nonexistent. However, this is not the case in superhero comics; since at least the 1960s, "the industry seems to be unique in that a lot of creative people have started out as fans" (Pearson and Uricchio 31).[16] Creators and editors in the comic book industry have themselves mostly been former fans who grew up reading superhero comics. Though the chances of being hired as a professional contributor remain small, in superhero comics, the line between producer and fan is an arbitrary boundary that is crossed every day at DC and Marvel work desks. For superhero comics, fandom is also working inside the publishing house.

In a discussion of her writing, Gail Simone notes that "[t]here's a thing I call the 'Batmobile Moment.' Nearly every pro writer who gets the chance [to write comics] experiences it, it's that first time you write the word 'Batmobile' in a script and you realize, holy crap, I'm writing Batman (or whomever)" (Wickline). This Batmobile Moment, a moment in which comic book writers find themselves in the position to officially write for a property for which they are also a fan, places this fan-turned-pro in a unique position. With the stroke of a pen—and with approval of an editor—fanon, or even that fan-turned-pro's unique headcanons, can become canon.[17] While other forms of mass media might view participatory fandom as a threat to the producers' authorial and interpretative control, it is an undeniable reality that superhero comics rely on fandom not only for its revenue streams but for its continued viability as a creative storytelling enterprise.

Conclusion

As demonstrated in this chapter, fandom has a unique relationship to the superhero comics industry. While early television and film fandoms often had antagonistic relationships with the producers of their favored texts, the growth of a comics fandom was encouraged by comic book publishers at several stages in its development, in privileging and rewarding fan commentary as well as encouraging the formation of early fan clubs. This encouragement helped kick-start the fandom, which, by following the practices of fan analysis and creative interpretation via headcanons, fanfiction, and fanon utilized by fandoms in general, allowed fans of superhero comics to act as cowriters who expanded and transformed the world of superheroes alongside the canon sources that served as their inspiration. At this point, with many professional industry creators being former fans themselves who bring their own views as a fan into their production of the canon, the boundaries between producer and consumer are blurred to the point that they may cease to exist at all. Perhaps more than any other mass media industry, fans of superhero comics are as much coauthors of the official text as the professional creators whose works inspired them.

CONCLUSION

As the preceding chapters illustrate, artistic collaboration, including the influences of corporate control and fan creativity, affects mainstream superhero comics in every step of its creation and reception. While the nominal writer, thanks to the "myth of the solitary genius" (Stillinger 22), has been credited as the arbiter of all writing decisions in comics scholarship, this is simply not the case. In mainstream superhero comics, corporate copyright holders can demand fundamental alterations to a writer's vision as well as extend the final creation's publication life in direct opposition to said writer's wishes. Nominal writers often collaborate with nominal illustrators, allowing artists to make significant writing decisions that are difficult to delineate within the text without archival evidence or the testimony of the artists themselves. After an issue is published, any story elements may be revised, abandoned, or adapted at will by subsequent creators via retcons, or alternative histories can be introduced through multiversal counterparts. Similarly, through fandom conventions of creating headcanons and fanons, fans engage with and alter the text as a means of exploring creative possibilities, thereby transforming the collective understanding and reception of the original text. Thus, very little is actually under the sole creative control of a superhero comic's designated writer. The nature of mainstream superhero comics as a serial and collaborative popular medium, then, should fundamentally question our traditional notions of authorship as a singular enterprise, particularly within the context of new media. It should, instead, prompt us to embrace a more nuanced paradigm that gives acknowledgment to all actors who influence the development of the narrative as cocreators.

Though this book has illustrated numerous means through which collaborative authorship affects the creation and reception of superhero comics, there are still plentiful avenues for further examination and discussion. In the first two chapters, investigations of two influential writer–artist teams and their processes show that the collaborative process itself can affect the extent and recognizability of multiple authorship; examinations of other historical (or even contemporary active) creative teams could provide not only a better understanding of how the industry developed, but also how the circumstances of a creation process might affect the collaboration itself. Similar analysis of multiple authorship in other genres of comics (romance, mystery, horror, etc.) could also expand this view of collaborative authorship to other comics subgenres. Finally, explorations into the collaborative relationships between creators and other publishers—whether involving imprints of Marvel and DC (e.g., Vertigo Comics, Milestone Comics, Icon Comics, etc.), smaller companies (e.g., Dark Horse Comics), or independent publishers, or in comics industries outside of the United States (e.g., Japanese manga, French-Belgian bandes dessinées, etc.)—may provide a more nuanced understanding of the role of publishers and the industry in the creation of other varieties of comics. Through such study, future readers and scholars could ensure that the creative input of normally ignored contributors is given correct acknowledgment and credit. This would lead to a greater understanding of superhero comics—as an industry and an art form.

This book was the first to discuss the role of collaboration in comics as its primary subject. Hopefully, it is not the last. There is a bounty of information about superhero comics, but like the genre's continuity, it is nearly impossible for a single person to track all of its twists and turns. This book required deep and wide research.

However, it is the work of a single person, and this project has shown that something can become richer for having the acknowledged contributions and perspectives of others.

The world of superhero comics is abundant and its history rich; the universe of all comics as a medium is even vaster. There is so much more for us to learn.

ACKNOWLEDGMENTS

Although this book was an individual project, I would be remiss to suggest that it was completed without the support of others.

I am indebted to Dr. Robert Jackson for his encouragement of both me and this project in its original form at the University of Tulsa. Dr. Holly Laird and Dr. Sean Latham were invaluable in their support and suggestions.

I am thankful to the University of Tulsa's McFarlin Library staff, particularly Amanda Ferguson, Tamra Stansfield, and Terry Williams of Interlibrary Loans, for helping me find the resources I needed for this book's original drafting. Similarly, I am grateful for the resources of the Dayton Metro Library system for both the books and quiet study space I needed for revisions.

I thank the staff of University of Wyoming's American Heritage Center, who welcomed me into their archive and met my numerous retrieval requests with cheerful readiness.

Selections of what would become chapter 3 previously appeared in an article on *Modernism/modernity*'s Print Plus platform. I value the insights and editorial input of Matthew Levay and Rudrani Gangopadhyay as part of that process.

I am especially appreciative of the feedback given to me by Lisa McMurtray, Laura Strong, and Peter Tonguette of the University Press of Mississippi as well as by my peer reviewers.

I give special thanks to my parents, Bob and Sharie Sartain, and my brother, Frank. Their support has made so much possible.

Last, but not least, I will be forever grateful to my husband, Steven Carpenter, for his constant support. He was my cheerleader through every stage of this project. His encouragement and belief in me have kept me going, and they always will.

NOTES

Chapter 1: Who Cowrote the *Watchmen?*: Alan Moore, Multiple Authorship, and Convergence Culture

1. These characters have since been folded into DC Comics' roster of characters.

2. For more on how these reversals take place, see chapter 3.

3. In case readers did not immediately see the Big Blue Boy Scout in the emotionless Dr. Manhattan, *Watchmen* explicitly invokes the DC Comics character. When Dr. Manhattan's existence is revealed to the world, a news reporter announces that "the superman *exists*, and he's *American*" (Moore et al. *Watchmen* 4.13.1, emphasis original). To add an extra note of existential terror, the supplemental material for the Manhattan-centric issue, which takes the form of a report on Dr. Manhattan's effect on the Cold War powers, says that the reporters who adopted that sound bite misquoted the author: "What I said was '*God* exists and he's American'" (Moore et al., *Watchmen* 4, Sup. 2).

This does not mean, however, that all traces of Charlton Comics were erased from the new *Watchmen* characters. In Dr. Malcolm Long's psychological profile of Rorschach/Walter Kovacs, it is mentioned that a young Walter Kovacs was removed from his mother's home and spent the rest of his childhood in the Lillian Charlton Home for Problem Children (Moore et al. Sup. 2), perhaps paying homage to the fact that the Charlton characters had likewise lost their childhood home of the soon-to-close Charlton Comics.

4. In the digital age, most mainstream comics are typically directly drawn and lettered in computer art programs. The jobs of penciler and inker are now usually combined into the singular role of "artist". This designation, in my opinion, downplays the artistic contribution of colorists, who still hold a separate position, particularly because, as Gibbons notes, "*although theirs is the final contribution, it has the first impact on the reader. Bad coloring can kill artwork and obscure story*" (164, emphasis original). "Line artist" would be a more appropriate title.

5. Gibbons used a Gillott 1068A pen for outlines, which creates a very uniform line. This choice visually separated *Watchmen* from its superhero comic contemporaries, which tended to have a brushstroke-like style for outlining (Gibbons 70).

6. According to Gibbons, Moore introduced the Gordian Knot Lock Company to the story without thinking about the connection between Alexander the Great and Veidt/Ozymandias (Gibbons 204). A Watsonian analysis would surmise that perhaps the locksmith is somehow one of Veidt's nebulous business entanglements; a Doylist perspective would suggest that Moore may not have told Gibbons about it yet, or was at least subconsciously thinking about Alexander the Great's influence on Veidt while writing the script for issue 3 (Moore et al., *Watchmen* 3.8.1), the company's first appearance.

7. This feeling, however, does not last for long, as Juspeczyk and Dr. Manhattan return to New York to find the aftermath of Veidt's faked alien invasion (Moore et al., *Watchmen* 12.7.1–2). Even if Juspeczyk convinced Dr. Manhattan that life on Earth was worth protecting when they were on Mars, this conviction quickly dissolves when Dr. Manhattan decides to leave the Milky Way galaxy "for one less complicated" (Moore et al., *Watchmen* 12.27.3). In the recent *Doomsday Clock* sequel miniseries, to which Moore is very opposed, Dr. Manhattan has found himself more at home in the traditional DC Comics universe, though it would be difficult to argue that world is less complex than the world of *Watchmen*.

8. This conversion into a bound book was not completely done without consultation from the *Watchmen* creative team, as Gibbons designed the cover of Watchmen for the bound "graphic novel" version (Gibbons 244–45).

9. While *Watchmen* is technically a trade paperback (or, in more recent collections, a hardback), it was also one of the first to be called a graphic novel (Gibbons 237), though this distinction is perhaps splitting hairs, as trade paperbacks in general are increasingly referred to as graphic novels. I am personally reticent to use the term "graphic novel," as it has problematic connotations. The term was created for adults who did not wish to seem immature and uncultured when discussing their creating and/or reading comics—a stigma that once affected now-famous greats such as Stan Lee and Neil Gaiman (Moore et al., *Watchmen: The Annotated Edition* 7, no. 8; Frakes et al.). They do not deal with comics (those are, after all, only for children); instead, they read and write novels featuring a lot of pictures. But would one be reticent to say one is a movie director or moviegoer, despite most mainstream films being created to be enjoyed by minors and families? To accept the term "graphic novel," in my mind, is to accept that there is some aspect of other, non-graphic-novel comics that is unworthy of cultural and intellectual consideration, something that necessitates an apologia. But even that question belies a larger, more cutting question: even if comics were, by their intrinsic nature, always and forever for children, why should we as consumers of media allow the optics of respectability, of seeming

mature and refined in all aspects of presentation, to diminish something that brings us joy and insight by claiming it is something else? I will happily stick with my comic books.

10. Oddly for a creator who is so protective of his works and any adaptations thereof, Moore has never revealed misgivings about the continued printing of *Watchmen* in a bound volume as such, despite its alteration from the format in which *Watchmen* was initially conceived. Instead, his contention appears to be with the fact that each subsequent reprinting of *Watchmen* in graphic novel format extends DC's ownership of the property. It is not that he disapproves of the continued printing of his work as a bound volume, it seems; it is that it is done without his permission and, in the process, continues to keep the rights to *Watchmen* out of his reach.

Moore is not alone in his condemnation of treating comic books as storyboards for films; see, for example, Will Eisner's discussion of the differences between visual storytelling in comics versus films (71–73).

11. While Gibbons notes that *Watchmen* struggled to keep up with production schedules (70), such delays would likely have lasted vastly longer if Moore had acted as both writer and artist.

12. In his annotated edition of *Watchmen*, Leslie Klinger suggests that the journal the police confiscated from Rorschach was impossible to read because of Rorschach's use of a personal shorthand, and that the presence of a more readable "final draft" indicates his intentions to have the journal published at some point (Moore et al., *Watchmen: The Annotated Edition* 322), further cementing the image of Rorschach as an authorial figure.

Chapter 2: Marvel Madness: Stan Lee and the "Marvel Method"

1. Chris Hatfield argues against this common description of Marvel's characters having "realistic" problems, arguing that the Marvel approach to characterization "was comparatively realistic, but only for the sake of anchoring the elements of the bizarre, otherworldly, gargantuan, and operatic that played just as big a part in the Marvel aesthetic" (Hatfield 121). Similarly, Alan Moore has described this approach to character creation as "two-dimensional characterization" even as he acknowledges that "at the time this was breathtakingly innovative and seemed a perfectly good way of producing comics that had relevance to the times in which they were being produced" (Moore and Burrows 23).

2. For an extensive list of Lee's television and film appearances, see his IMDb page ("Stan Lee").

3. While this is the most commonly used name for this process, it is not universal. Dennis O'Neil, for example, refers to this method as the "plot-first method" (31).

4. True to form, this memoir takes the form of a comic book and is cowritten with Peter David, with line art by Colleen Doran and colors by Bill Farmer, with Val Trullinger, Juan Fernandez, Joseph Baker, and Jose Villarubia. It does not contain page numbers.

5. To confound this shortage further, in the 1970s Marvel attempted to over-whelm DC on the stands by introducing a new series every month (Raphael and Spurgeon 146).

6. For an extended discussion of how comics companies such as Marvel worked to cultivate a participatory fan culture by elevating fan feedback, see chapter 4.

7. The brevity of this synopsis as the first stage of writing in the Marvel Method is what leads some comics studies scholars such as Charles Hatfield to describe Lee and others acting as writers using the Marvel Method as "scenarists" instead (Hatfield 90–91).

8. The length of a comic book has varied greatly over the course of the medi-um's history. In the 1930s, a Timely comic book was about sixty-eight pages long, including multiple stories as well as the two full-text pages required to qualify for a magazine's postage rate. Today, a Marvel comic is about twenty pages (Cronin, "How Many Pages Long Have Marvel Comic Stories Been Over the Years?").

9. Writer Bob Kane was long given full credit for creating the Batman char-acter in 1939, denying cocreator and illustrator Bill Finger proper attribution and attendant royalties. For a discussion of the controversy and the struggle to give Finger the credit he deserved, see Dan Argott, Brooke Blair, Will Blair, and Demian Fenton's documentary *Batman & Bill: A Secret Identity Finally Revealed* (Argott et al.).

10. Even after he came back to the *Batman* comic books, Kane hired his coworkers to act as ghostwriters without DC's knowledge (Moldoff 16).

11. Every person who appears or is mentioned in the recording, besides pro-duction manager Sol Brodski, has been given a Lee-style nickname. To listen to the unscripted recording, see "Stan Lee and the Voices of Marvel—For Members of 'The Merry Marvel Marching Society'" (Media Mix Comics).

12. For a more extensive discussion of the use of multiverses, see chapter 3.

13. For a more extensive discussion of continuity, see chapter 3.

14. The overt performance of 1970s masculinity is evident throughout the Stan Lee Papers. Among his various brainstorms for non-Marvel publications, which he engaged in throughout his career, is hand-drawn concept art for a pornographic photo book titled *Fannies*, featuring close-up views of (presumably female) buttocks (Stan Lee, *Fannies*).

15. With Lee's relatively recent death, further materials may be added to the Stan Lee Papers at a later date, or some other collection might become available for public viewing. However, because I am not an expert in estate management, I cannot predict when such additions (if they exist) might be incorporated into

the existing archive. Until presented with contradicting evidence, I am writing under the assumption that the Stan Lee Papers at the American Heritage Center represent the entirety of Lee's collection of extant Marvel Method artifacts.

16. Solarman was originally published by Pendulum Press from 1979 to 1980.

17. The character was later revived by Scout Comics in a creator-owned *Solarman* series from 2016 to 2017.

18. Although Stan and Joan Lee had one daughter, Joan Celia, in 1960, they wanted to have more children. However, after their second daughter, Jan, died three days after birth in 1963, the Lees were informed that they were no longer able to have biological children (Lee, David et al.; Frakes et al.). Additionally, due to the mixed religions within the Lee household (Stan Jewish, Joan Episcopalian) they were legally unable to adopt further children. In their documentary of Lee's life, Nikki Frakes, Terry Douglas, and Will Hess suggest this incident partially motivated Lee's increased creation of characters who were affected by systemic oppression such as the Black Panther, the Falcon, and the X-Men (Frakes et al.).

19. The document is titled "Synopses" despite being singular (Lee, *Synposes: The Fantastic Four July '61 Schedule*). Instead of including a "[*sic*]" after each citation of this document, I acknowledge in this note this is a spelling error on Lee's part, not my own.

20. Bendis notes, though, that while the style of the script is largely up to the writer and is not mandated by the overarching company, "[g]enerally, in today's market, most comic writers write something close to [a] full script. Even those applying a Marvel Style method use more detail than previous generations did" (Bendis 28).

21. The Human Torch of *Fantastic Four* fame was based on Carl Burgos's fiery android The Torch, which appeared in the 1939 *Marvel Comics* #1, the series after which the company later named itself. See Reed and David Lee et al. This robotic inspiration perhaps explains the emphasis on the "human" aspect of "the Human Torch."

22. Following *Fantastic Four* #284, published November 1985, Sue Storm's superhero alias was changed from Invisible Girl to Invisible Woman.

23. This problem was avoided in the published version of *Fantastic Four* #1 by allowing Invisible Girl's clothes to become invisible along with her. In *Fantastic Four* #3, Sue designs the team's iconic power-compatible jumpsuits (Lee, Kirby, Brodsky et al.), though it is unclear which member of the creative team originated the idea.

24. While Lee was officially Marvel Comics' publisher at the time, Lee claims to Workman that he is not even sure which "powers-that-be" at Marvel headquarters he should relay these concerns to, "what with all the personnel changes lately" (Workman). From this note, it is difficult to determine if Lee is sincere in not knowing the current roster of Marvel executives or if he is merely making excuses.

25. Lee's noted insistence on expressive drawings may be influenced by the melodramatic silent movies he enjoyed as a child (Frakes et al.).

26. Ditko claims to have written rough dialogue on separate sheets of paper when using the Marvel Method (Raphael and Spurgeon 91); however, I could not find evidence of this during my visit to the archive.

27. While Lee suggests in his script that the Hulk blend into the background to make the civilians' inability to spot the brightly colored antihero more plausible, this recommendation was not carried out. In the final issue, the character is easily visible in all his bright green glory against a backdrop of downed brown trees and seafoam green. Whether this was because coloring was already underway when Macchio received the script, Macchio did not see this as important enough to emphasize with colorist Paul Becton, or Becton took artistic license is impossible to determine.

28. This rampage is stopped by Thor during the issue's climax (S. Lee, *Thor Special*).

29. The creators credited by last name on the cover of this issue are, in order, James Felder (who acted as writer), Sal Buscema (penciler), Steve Ditko (penciler), Dick Ayers (penciler and inker), Gil Kane (penciler), Tom Palmer (inker) Al Migrom (inker), and Steve Leialoha (inker). Also not listed on the cover are letterer John Costanza and editor Joe Andreani.

Chapter 3: Which Earth Is This Again?: The Retcon vs. The Multiverse

1. With a June 1938 cover date.

2. This was, of course, before the death of superheroes (and their almost inevitable resurrection) became a not uncommon occurrence in the genre.

3. For a more in-depth discussion of how DC and Marvel encourage fan engagement and developed the current detail-oriented fandom, see chapter 4.

4. See, for example, *Old Man Logan* (2015, 2016–18), *Old Man Hawkeye* (2018), *Old Man Quill* (2019) ("A to Z in Marvel Comic Series"). Frank Tieri and Mauricet made reference to this trend as part of their *Harley Quinn* run for DC Comics in issue #42, which showed an apocalyptic future featuring "Old Lady Harley" (Tieri and Mauricet).

5. The exact number of Robins and a list of their identities are matters of debate, depending on one's approach. Depending on how one treats retcons and multiverses, there have been anywhere between four and eight official Robins. If one includes We Are Robin—a youth vigilante group that forms in Gotham after the apparent death of Batman (Bermejo et al.)—the number may reach eighteen.

6. For how such letter-writing sections were used to encourage reader engagement and participation, see chapter 4.

7. For more information regarding how comic book companies encouraged this orientation to detail and accurate memory, see chapter 4.

8. In the DC animated cartoon *Justice League Unlimited*, The Question is triumphant when he discovers a thirty-second flavor as part of his investigations (Dos Santos). The ice cream company is not named, but the reference is clear.

9. In the comic, Allen states that in his world the Jay Garrick comics were written by Gardner Fox, actual cocreator of Garrick and writer of *The Flash* #123 (Fox et al. 9); Fox-through-Allen suggests that his writing "tuned in" to Garrick's Earth; thus, all of the previously written adventures were real (Fox et al.). When Allen returns to his original Earth, he plans in the issue's final panel to find Fox and tell him the tale, so "[h]e can write the whole thing up in a comic book!" (Fox et al. 25). This tongue-in-cheek use of metanarrative is common when the multiverse is invoked in superhero comics.

10. On a few occasions, Marvel Comics and DC Comics have published crossover titles, such as *Superman vs. The Amazing Spider-Man: The Battle of the Century* (1976), *Batman & Captain America* (1996), and in *The Amalgam Age of Comics* (1996), DC and Marvel characters were merged. DC Comics has not named these universes as part of their official listing, but Marvel purports that Superman fought Spider-Man in Earth-7642 (Carter), Batman and Captain America teamed up to defeat the Joker and the Red Skull in Earth-3839 (Carter), and has listed the Amalgam Universe as both Earth-692 and Earth-9602 (*Amalgam Index*).

11. For the best comprehensive source for all series within the Ultimates Universe and their relative timelines, see Julian Darius's cataloguing for Sequart Organization's Continuity Pages (Darius).

12. DC Comics has a similar imprint, Earth-1, in which classic characters like Superman, Wonder Woman, and Batman "are just starting out" ("Earth-1"). However, this lasted only a year, beginning in 2010 and ending in 2011.

13. At least for me, this turned out to be the case; my first comic book was *Ultimate Spider-Man* #9.

14. Although not explicitly claimed as part of a DC Comics universe, Wonder Woman's iconic skirt and boots are presented as Superman (whose calves are visible), and she warns that this universe is "private property" (Kibblesmith et al. 15).

15. Hailing from Earth-8311, Peter Porker was a spider bitten by a radioactive pig, transforming him into an anthropomorphic pig with the powers classically associated with Spider-Man.

16. Spider-Ma'am is a version of May Parker, Peter Parker's aunt, who gained spider-powers instead of her nephew.

17. Spiders-Man is a cluster of spiders that absorbed the consciousness of Peter Parker in the radiation experiment that granted the original Spider-Man his powers.

18. The *White Knight* universe—consisting of the *Batman: White Knight* (2017–18) and multiple sequels/spinoff series—follows a universe in which the

Joker temporarily regained sanity and sought to show Gotham that Batman is the true villain, as well as the consequences of this crusade.

19. Comics writer Grant Morrison has a much harsher view of this decision, claiming that *Crisis on Infinite Earths* was "elegiac continuity audit made to purge all story meat that was seen as too strong for the tender palates of an imagined new generation who would need believable and grounded hero books" (Morrison 214).

Chapter 4: Sharing the Sandbox: Corporate Interests and Fandoms

1. The term "grok," meaning loosely "to understand deeply and instinctually" or "to resonate with on a fundamental level," is a neologism from Robert A. Heinlein's 1961 novel *Stranger in a Strange Land*. Its use here signals that these fans are deeply entrenched in science fiction fandom, and that they highly relate to the character.

2. As Jean-Paul Gabilliet notes, "Comics fandom was born in the bosom of science fiction fandom but it established a close relationship to the comic book format from the start" (258).

3. For a brief history of Marvel's evolution as a company leading up to this period, see chapter 2.

4. For a more detailed discussion regarding the evolution of continuity in superhero comics, see chapter 3.

5. For an example of a Marvel No-Prize, see Stan Lee Papers Box 127 Folder 10: "Envelopes—Marvel No-Prize (with Spider-Man), 1996" (Marvel Entertainment Group).

6. In his 2015 memoir, Stan Lee reported that "to this day, I sometimes go to a business meeting and someone takes out a tattered old *No-Prize* envelope he received years ago and asks me to sign it" (Lee, David, et al., emphasis original).

7. See, for example, Weaver (48).

8. This need to preserve the utility of the company's properties is a major impetus for DC Comics' rejection of Alan Moore's initial proposal to create *Watchmen* using characters recently purchased from the now-defunct Charleton Comics, instead requiring Moore and Dave Gibbons to create a whole new set of characters. For a further explanation, see chapter 1.

9. The similarities that Jenkins noted between fan and academic textual analysis may stem from the fact that, until as late as 2004, the fan groups that were studied by early fan scholars were believed to be comprised of "straight women" who were "overeducated for their jobs" (Busse 159; Jenkins, *Textual Poachers* 282). Fans, then, could be seen as applying a modified form of analysis learned in academic settings to their fan interests.

10. Offensive characterizations of female characters are, unfortunately, not uncommon, and can range from drawing women in impossible "broke back"

contortions to show off both breasts and buttocks (see Cocca) to treating their characters as accessories to male characters to subjecting female characters to "fridging"—the tendency for superheroines and other female characters to be "*either depowered, raped, or cut up and stuck in the refrigerator*" as means of furthering a male character's storyline (Simone, emphasis original). Simone's final example refers to *Green Lantern* #53 (1994), in which a supervillain breaks into the apartment of the titular hero (Kyle Rainer, one of several Green Lanterns), murders his girlfriend, and leaves her dismembered corpse in the refrigerator for him to find (Marz et al.).

11. When discussing this dynamic, Jenkins explicitly refers to women having to navigate a media environment largely designed to appeal to male reader/viewers (Jenkins, *Textual Poachers* 112–15). However, though *Textual Poachers*, like most early fan studies works, was "defined around female experiences and pleasures" (Jenkins and Scott xi), this relationship to the predominant media norms could easily be applied to other groups, such as LGBTQ+ people or people of color. The following interactions with the canon in terms of headcanons, fanons, and fanfiction, in any case, have become more mainstream than when Jenkins described this dynamic in 1992.

12. Superman ice cream is a variety of ice cream popular in the Midwestern United States. Although recipes and exact flavors vary, it is a mixture of red, yellow, and blue ice cream reminiscent of the character's costume.

13. Fan fiction is also referred to as "fanfiction" or "fanfic," depending on the writer's personal preference. I will use these versions of the term interchangeably.

14. Busse notes that this is not a property unique to fan fiction, as "much of [literature] is citational, referencing and alluding to earlier texts" (Busse 114).

15. The reasons a fan's metatext may suggest this include but are not limited to the murder of his parents and his stated belief that "[a gun] is the weapon of the *enemy*. We do not *need* it. We will not *use* it" (Miller et al., emphasis original).

16. Friedenthal points to former English teacher Roy Thomas, who joined Marvel Comics as editor in 1965, as the first to become what he calls a "fanturned-pro" (Friedenthal 33–34).

17. At least, until it is retconned by the next creative team (see chapter 3).

BIBLIOGRAPHY

"A to Z in Marvel Comic Series." *Marvel Entertainment*. https://www.marvel. com/comics/series. Accessed 17 August 2020.

Abad-Santos, Alex. "The Darker Side of Stan Lee's Legacy: Honoring Lee's Legacy at Marvel Means Honoring the People He Worked with." *Vox*, 17 November 2018. https://www.vox.com/2016/2/23/11098942/stan-lee-death-marvel-legacy.

Amalgam Index. http://www.marvunapp.com/list/amalgamd.htm. Accessed 15 October 2020.

Argott, Don, Brooke Blair, Will Blair, and Demian Fenton. *Batman & Bill: A Secret Identity Finally Revealed*. Wiesbaden KSM Gmbh, 2019.

Augustyn, Brian, Mike Mignola, P. Craig Russell, and Robert Bloch. *Gotham by Gaslight: A Tale of the Batman*. DC Comics, 1989.

Ayres, Jackson. "Writing for the Trade or Writing for a Trade?" *Inks: The Journal of the Comics Studies Society* 5, no. 3 (2021): 239–60.

Baetens, Jan. "Adaptation: A Writerly Strategy?" In *Comics and Adaptations*, edited by Benoît Mitaine et al., translated by Aarnoud Rommens and David Roche, 31–46. University Press of Mississippi, 2018.

Barthes, Roland. "From Work to Text." In *Image, Music, Text*, edited by Stephen Heath, translated by Stephen Heath, 155–64. Hill and Wang, 1977.

Barthes, Roland. *S/Z: An Essay*. Translated by Richard Miller. Hill and Wang, 1974.

Beck, Jackson, Bud Collyer, and Joan Alexander. *The Adventures of Superman*. 8 May 2018. *Internet Archive*. http://archive.org/details/TheAdventuresOf Superman_201805.

Behring, John, director. "Birds of Prey." *Arrow*, 40, CW Network, 26 March 2014.

Bendis, Brian Michael. *Words for Pictures: The Art and Business of Writing Comics and Graphic Novels*. Watson-Guptill Publications, 2014.

Benjamin, Walter. *The Work of Art in the Age of Its Technological Reproducibility, and Other Writings on Media*. Edited by Michael W. Jennings, Brigid Doherty, and Thomas Y. Levin, translated by Edmund Jephcott, Rodney Livingstone, Howard Eiland et al. Harvard University Press, 2008.

Bermejo, Lee, Khary Randolph, Jorge Corona, Rob Haynes, Patricia Mulvihill, and Ken Lopez. *We Are Robin #1*. DC Comics, 2015.

Bredehoft, Thomas A. "Style, Voice, and Authorship in Harvey Pekar's (Auto) (Bio)Graphical Comics." *College Literature: A Journal of Critical Literary Studies* 38, no. 3 (Summer 2011): 97–110.

Bunn, Cullen, Salva Espin, Veronica Gandini, and Joe Sabino. *Deadpool Kills Deadpool*. Marvel Comics, 2013.

Busse, Kristina. *Framing Fan Fiction: Literary and Social Practices in Fan Fiction Communities*. University of Iowa Press, 2017.

"Captain Atom (Allen Adam) (Character)." *Comic Vine*. https://comicvine.gamespot.com/captain-atom-allen-adam/4005-96401/. Accessed 1 September 2019.

Carter, Madison. "Earth-Crossover (Alternate Earth)." *Appendix to the Handbook of the Marvel Universe*, 2008. http://www.marvunapp.com/Appendix3/earthcrossoverall.htm.

Cates, Donny, Ryan Stegman, Joshua Cassara, Frank Martin, and Vc Clayton Cowles. *Venom #11*. Marvel Comics, 2019.

Cieply, Michael. "Ruling Gives Heirs a Share of Superman Copyright." *New York Times*, 29 March 2008. https://www.nytimes.com/2008/03/29/business/media/29comics.html.

Clark, Josh. "Do Parallel Universes Really Exist?" *HowStuffWorks*, 17 October 2007. https://science.howstuffworks.com/science-vs-myth/everyday-myths/parallel-universe.htm.

Cocca, Carolyn. "The 'Broke Back Test': A Quantitative and Qualitative Analysis of Portrayals of Women in Mainstream Superhero Comics, 1993–2013." *Journal of Graphic Novels and Comics* 5, no. 4 (October 2014): 411–28.

"Comic-Book Time." *TV Tropes*. https://tvtropes.org/pmwiki/pmwiki.php/Main/ComicBookTime. Accessed 17 August 2020.

Consequences of Sound. "'BREAKING: #StanLee, the Single Greatest Contributor to Comic Book Culture and Creativity in the History of the Format, Has Died at the Age of 95 https://T.Co/C53dqWxQeL'/Twitter." https://twitter.com/consequence/status/1062054578114494464. Accessed 10 November 2019.

Cooke, Jon B. *Toasting Absent Heroes: Alan Moore Discusses the Charlton-Watchmen Connection*, no. 9 (Apr. 2009). http://www.twomorrows.com/comicbookartist/articles/09moore.html.

Coppa, Francesca. "Writing Bodies in Space: Media Fan Fiction as Theatrical Performance." In *The Fan Fiction Studies Reader*, edited by Karen Hellekson and Kristina Busse, 218–37. University of Iowa Press, 2014.

Cronin, Brian. "Comic Book Legends Revealed #373." *CBR*, 29 June 2012. https://www.cbr.com/comic-book-legends-revealed-373/.

Cronin, Brian. "Comic Book Urban Legends Revealed #12!" *CBR*, 18 August 2005. https://www.cbr.com/comic-book-urban-legends-revealed-12/.

Cronin, Brian. "How Many Pages Long Have Marvel Comic Stories Been Over the Years?" *CBR*, 14 August 2017. https://www.cbr.com/marvel-comics-how-many-pages-long/.

Daniels, Les. *Batman: The Life and Times of the Dark Knight: The Complete History*. Chronicle Books, 1999.

Daniels, Les. *DC Comics: A Celebration of the World's Favorite Comic Book Heroes*. Billboard Books, 2003.

Darius, Julian. "The Continuity Pages: Marvel's Ultimate Universe." *Sequart Organization*, n.d. http://sequart.org/continuity-pages/ultimate-marvel/.

David, Peter, Greg Land, Jay Leisten, and Frank D'Armata. *Symbiote Spider-Man: Alien Reality #5*. Marvel Comics, 2020.

DC Comics. *DC Focus*. Comic-Con International, San Diego.

DeFalco, Tom. *To the DEATH—!*, 997. Stan Lee Papers, Box 65, Folder 2.

DeForest, Tim. "Marvel Comics." *Encyclopedia Britannica*, 7 March 2019. https://www.britannica.com/topic/Marvel-Comics.

Ditko, Steve. "Why I Quit S-M, Marvel." *Four-Page Series*, no. 9 (2015).

Dos Santos, Joaquim, director. "Grudge Match." *Justice League Unlimited*, 35. Cartoon Network, March 11 2006.

"Earth-1." *DC*, 19 February 2015. https://www.dccomics.com/characters/earth-1.

Eco, Umberto. "The Myth of Superman." In *Arguing Comics: Literary Masters on a Popular Medium*, edited by Jeet Heer and Kent Worcester, 146–64. University Press of Mississippi, 2004.

Eisner, Will. *Graphic Storytelling and Visual Narrative*. Poorhouse Press.

Ellis, John. *Visible Fictions*. Routledge & Kegan Paul, 1982.

Ennis, Garth, et al. *John Constantine, Hellblazer #63*. Edited by Stuart Moore. DC Comics, 1993.

Everett, Larry. "The Soapbox: The Problem with Power Creep and Progression." *Engadget*. https://www.engadget.com/2012-11-06-the-soapbox-the-problem-with-power-creep-and-progression.html. Accessed 17 August 2020.

Felder, James. *Legend and Heroes #2 Plot: "Avengers Assemble!,"* 1997. Stan Lee Papers, Box 51, Folder 12.

Fox, Gardner, Carmine Infantino, and Joe Giella. *The Flash #123: Flash of Two Worlds*. DC Comics, 1961.

Fox, Gardner, and Joe Kubert. *The Brave and the Bold #31*. National Comics, 1961.

Frakes, Nikki, Terry Dougas, and Will Hess. *With Great Power: The Stan Lee Story*. https://www.youtube.com/watch?v=Ct9VTQnPa5c&t=1865s&has_verified=1. Accessed 9 April 2019.

Freedland, Nat. "Super Heroes with Super Problems." *New York Herald Tribune*, 9 January 1966, p. n.p.

Friedenthal, Andrew J. *Retcon Game: Retroactive Continuity and the Hyperlinking of America*. University Press of Mississippi, 2017.

Gabilliet, Jean-Paul. *Of Comics and Men: A Cultural History of American Comic Books*. Translated by Bart Beaty and Nick Nguyen. University Press of Mississippi, 2010.

Garcia-López, José Luis, Jerry Ordway, Jim Lee, Clay Mann, Rafael Albuquerque, Richard Donner, Curt Swan, Patrick Gleason, Olivier Coipel, John Cassaday, Neal Adams, Jakub Syty, Peter J. Tomasi, Marv Wolfman, Geoff Johns, Scott Snyder, Tom King, Louise Simonson, Paul Dini, Brad Meltzer, Brian Michael Bendis, Paul Levitz, Dan Jurgenss, and Egmont Polska. *Action Comics* #100. DC Comics, 2019.

Gardner, Eriq. "Warner Bros.' 'Superman' Rights Confirmed by Appeals Court." *Hollywood Reporter*, 10 February 2016. https://www.hollywoodreporter.com /thr-esq/warner-bros-superman-rights-confirmed-864026.

Gardner, Jared. "Film + Comics: A Multimodal Romance in the Age of Transmedial Convergence." In *Storyworlds across Media: Toward a Media-Conscious Narratology*, edited by Marie-Laure Ryan and Jan-Noël Thon, 193–310. University of Nebraska Press, 2014.

Gibbons, Dave. *Watching the Watchmen*. Edited by Chip Kidd and Mike Essl. Titan Books, 2008.

Gibbs, John, et al. *Solarman*. Marvel Productions.

Goggin, Joyce, and Dan Hassler-Forest. "Introduction: Out of the Gutter: Reading Comics and Graphic Novels." In *The Rise and Reason of Comics and Graphic Literature: Critical Essays on the Form*, edited by Joyce Goggin and Dan Hassler-Forest, 1–4. McFarland & Company, 2010.

Gordon, Ian. *Superman: The Persistence of an American Icon*. Rutgers University Press, 2017.

Groensteen, Thierry. *The System of Comics*. University Press of Mississippi, 2007.

Grossberg, Lawrence. "The Indifference of Television, or, Mapping TV's Popular (Affective) Economy." In *Dancing in Spite of Myself: Essays on Popular Culture*, 125–44. Duke University Press, 1997.

Grossman, Lev. "All-TIME 100 Novels." *Time*. http://entertainment.time. com/2005/10/16/all-time-100-novels/slide/watchmen-1986-by-alan-moore-dave-gibbons/. Accessed 20 September 2019.

"Grudge Match." *Justice League Unlimited*, directed by Joaquim Dos Santos, season 3, episode 9, Cartoon Network, 2006.

Gruenwald, Mark. "Mark's Remarks." *The Avengers* #269, Marvel Comics, 1986.

Gruenwald, Mark. "Mark's Remarks." *The West Coast Avengers* #10, Marvel Comics, 1986.

"Grudge Match." *Justice League Unlimited*, directed by Joaquim Dos Santos, 35, Cartoon Network, 11 March 2006.

Hellekson, Karen, and Kristina Busse. "Fan Communities and Affect." In *The Fan Fiction Studies Reader*, edited by Karen Hellekson and Kristina Busse, 131–37. University of Iowa Press, 2014.

Hellekson, Karen, and Kristina Busse. "Fan Fiction as Literature." *The Fan Fiction Studies Reader*, edited by Karen Hellekson and Kristina Busse, 19–25. University of Iowa Press, 2014.

Hembeck, Fred. "The Fred Hembeck Show: Episode 21." *IGN*, 26 June 2012. https://www.ign.com/articles/2005/08/02/ the-fred-hembeck-show-episode-21.

Itzkoff, Dave. "The Vendetta Behind 'V for Vendetta.'" *New York Times*, 12 March 2006. https://www.nytimes.com/2006/03/12/movies/the-vendetta-behind-v -for-vendetta.html.

Jenkins, Henry. *Convergence Culture: Where Old and New Media Collide*. New York University Press, 2006.

Jenkins, Henry. *Textual Poachers: Television Fans and Participatory Culture*, updated twentieth anniversary edition. Routledge, 2013.

Jenkins, Henry, and Suzanne Scott. "Textual Poachers: Twenty Years Later: A Conversation between Henry Jenkins and Suzanne Scott." In *Textual Poachers: Television Fans and Participatory Culture*, updated twentieth anniversary edition, vii–1. Routledge, 2013.

Johnson, Derek. *Media Franchising: Creative License and Collaboration in the Culture Industries*. New York University Press, 2013.

Johnston, Rich. "Alan Moore and DC Comics – Then and Now." *Bleeding Cool News and Rumors*, 13 September 2010. https://www.bleedingcool.com/2010 /09/13/alan-moore-and-dc-comics-then-and-now/.

Kane, Bob and Bill Finger. *Detective Comics* #27. DC Comics, 1927.

Kibblesmith, Daniel, Carlos Villa, Roberto Poggi, and Chris O'Halloran. *Lockjaw #4: Vs. Annihilus!* Marvel Comics.

Koestenbaum, Wayne. *Double Talk: The Erotics of Male Literary Collaboration*. Routledge, 1989.

Kukkonen, Karin. "Navigating Infinite Earths: Readers, Mental Models, and the Multiverse of Superhero Comics." *Storyworlds: A Journal of Narrative Studies* 2, no. 1 (July 2010): 39–58.

Leader, Michael. "Dave Gibbons: Looking Back on the Watchmen Movie." *Den of Geek*, 22 July 2009. https://www.denofgeek.com/us/go/11388.

Lee, Jim. "In the Days When the Margins of the Art Was the Message Threads for Communicating Direction to Editors/Production Artists and Colorists! #youhadyourchancetobuythisforagrand #dontcrytome #artlifepic.Twitter. Com/W3J5EuTfJ2." @JimLee, 7 May 2019. https://twitter.com/JimLee/status /1125965108356608000.

Lee, Stan. *Are You Old Enough to Read Comicbooks?* 27 May 1975. Stan Lee Papers.

Lee, Stan. *Fannies*. c 1978. Stan Lee Papers, Box 53, Folder 4.

Lee, Stan. *Heroes and Legends: "Avengers Assemble!"* 1997. Stan Lee Papers, Box 51, Folder 12.

Lee, Stan. *Part Five: The Fiend Flies by Night!* 1977. Stan Lee Papers, Box 11, Folder 13.

Lee, Stan. *Solarman #2: "This Silent Death, This Hostage Earth" Script*. 1989. Stan Lee Papers, Box 57, Folder 4.

Lee, Stan. *Solarman #2: "This Silent Death, This Hostage Earth" Synopsis*. 1989. Stan Lee Papers, Box 57, Folder 4.

Lee, Stan. *Spider-Man (Kingpin) Special: "To the Death."* 1997. Stan Lee Papers, Box 65, Folder 2.

Lee, Stan. *Synposes: The Fantastic Four July '61 Schedule (#1)*. 1961. Stan Lee Papers, Box 51, Folder 7.

Lee, Stan. *Thor Special*. C. 1986. Stan Lee Papers, Box 66, Folder 13.

Lee, Stan, ed. *The Ultimate Silver Surfer*. Byron Preiss Multimedia Co.: Boulevard Books, 1995.

Lee, Stan, Jack Kirby, Dick Ayers, Stan Goldberg, and Artie Simek. Edited by Stan Lee. *Fantastic Four #11*. Marvel Comics.

Lee, Stan, Jack Kirby, George Klein, Christopher Rule, Stan Goldberg, and Artie Simek. Edited by Stan Lee. *Fantastic Four #1*. Marvel Comics, 1961.

Lee, Stan, Jack Kirby, Sol Brodsky, Stan Goldberg, and Artie Simek. *Fantastic Four #3*. Marvel Comics, 1961.

Lee, Stan, Jim Shooter, Eric Larsen, and Vince Colleta. *Be Thou God, or Monster!* c. 1986. Stan Lee Papers, Box 66, Folder 13.

Lee, Stan, John Buscema, and Rudy Nebres. *"The Answer" Annotated Pencils*. c. 1980. Stan Lee Papers, Box 55, Folder 8.

Lee, Stan, John Romita Sr., Tom DeFalco, Dan Green, and Steve Oliff. Ed. Ralph Macchio. *Spider-Man/Kingpin: To the Death*. Edited by Ralph Macchio, Marvel Comics, 1997. Stan Lee Papers, Box 65, Folder 2.

Lee, Stan, Peter David, Coleen Doran, Bill Farmer, Val Trullinger, Juan Fernandez, Joseph Baker, and Jose Villarubia. *Amazing, Fantastic, Incredible: A Marvelous Memoir*. Touchstone, 2015.

Lee, Stan, Steve Ditko, and Sam Rosen. "How Stan Lee and Steve Ditko Create Spider-Man!" In *The Amazing Spider Man Annual #1*, 38–40. Marvel Comics, 1964.

"Letter Columns (Concept)." *Comic Vine*. https://comicvine.gamespot.com/letter -columns/4015-56165/. Accessed 12 January 2021.

Levitz, Paul, and Liz Erickson, eds. *Detective Comics: 80 Years of Batman*. DC Comics, 2019.

"List of Current Marvel Comics Publications." *Wikipedia*, 2 July 2020. https://en.wikipedia.org/w/index. php?title=List_of_current_Marvel_Comics_publications&oldid=965607911.

Lopes, Paul. *Demanding Respect: The Evolution of the American Comic Book.* Temple University Press, 2009.

Manning, Shaun. "Alan Moore's Watchmen Feud with DC Comics, Explained." *CBR*, 25 November 2017. https://www.cbr.com/alan-moore-watchmen-feud -dc-comics-explained/.

Marvel Entertainment Group. *Congratulations!*, 1996. Stan Lee Papers, Box 127, Folder 10.

Marz, Ron. "Don't Wait, You Might Not Get Another Chance." *Messages from Marz.* http://ronmarz.com/2010/03/don't-wait-you-might-not-get-another -chance/. Accessed 29 August 2019.

Marz, Ron. *Green Lantern* #53. DC Comics, 1994.

McMillan, Graeme. "Gibbons: 'Before Watchmen' Is 'Not Really Watchmen.'" *ComicsAlliance*, 27 July 2012. https://comicsalliance.com/dave-gibbons -before-watchmen-not-really-watchmen/.

Media Mix Comics. *Stan Lee and the Voices of Marvel—for Members of "The Merry Marvel Marching Society."* https://www.youtube.com/watch?v=27g3u VUMqW8. Accessed 25 Apr. 2020.

Miettinen, Mervi. "Past as Multiple Choice—Textual Anarchy and the Problems of Continuity in Batman: The Killing Joke." *Scandinavian Journal of Comic Art* 1, no. 1 (2012): 3–25.

Millar, Mark, Dave Johnson, and Kilian Plunkett. *Superman: Red Son.* DC Comics, 2003.

Miller, Frank, Klaus Janson, Lynn Varley, and John Constanza. *Batman: The Dark Knight Returns* #4. DC Comics, 1986.

Moldoff, Sheldon. "'Maybe I Was Just Loyal: Longtime 'Batman' Artist SHELDON MOLDOFF Talks About Bob Kane and Other Phenomena." *Alter Ego*, no. 59 (June 2006).

Moore, Alan. *The Alan Moore Interview.* Interview by Gary Groth, 13 June 2012. http://www.tcj.com/the-alan-moore-interview-118/.

Moore, Alan, Dave Gibbons, and John Higgins. *Watchmen.* DC Comics, 2005.

Moore, Alan, Dave Gibbons, and John Higgins. *Watchmen: The Annotated Edition.* Edited by Leslie Klinger. DC Comics, 2017.

Moore, Alan, and Jacen Burrows. *Alan Moore's Writing for Comics.* Edited by William A. Christensen et al. Avatar Press, 2003.

Morrison, Grant. *Supergods: What Masked Vigilantes, Miraculous Mutants, and a Sun God from Smallville Can Teach Us About Being Human.* Spiegel & Grau, 2011.

Murphy, Sean, Todd Klein, and Matt Hollingsworth. *Batman: White Knight*, #1–8. DC Black Label, 2017–2018.

O'Neil, Dennis. *The DC Comics Guide to Writing Comics.* Watson-Guptill Publications, 2001.

Parsons, Patrick. "Batman and His Audience: The Dialectic of Culture." *The Many Lives of Batman: Critical Approaches to a Superhero and His Media*, edited by Roberta A. Pearson and William Uricchio, 66–89. Routledge, 1991.

Pearson, Roberta A., and William Uricchio. "Notes from the Batcave: An Interview with Dennis O'Neil." In *The Many Lives of Batman: Critical Approaches to a Superhero and His Media*, edited by Roberta A. Pearson and William Uricchio, 18–32. Routledge, 1991.

Planetary Names: Crater, Craters: Galle on Mars. https://planetarynames.wr.usgs.gov/Feature/2080. Accessed 10 September 2019.

Polo, Susana. "Allow Us To Explain: Alan Moore's Anti-DC Interview." *The Mary Sue*, 13 September 2010. https://www.themarysue.com/alan-moore-dc-comics-watchmen/.

Punday, Daniel. "Kavalier & Clay, the Comic-Book Novel, and Authorship in a Corporate World." *Critique: Studies in Contemporary Fiction* 49, no. 3 (Spring 2008): 291–302.

Raphael, Jordan, and Tom Spurgeon. *Stan Lee and the Rise and Fall of the American Comic Book*, first edition. Chicago Review Press, 2003.

"Real Fact Comics #3 (DC, 1946) Condition: VG+. VG+. H.G. Wells, Lon | Lot #15707." *Heritage Auctions*. https://comics.ha.com/itm/golden-age-1938–1955-/non-fiction/real-fact-comics-3-dc-1946-condition-vg-vg-hg-wells-lon-chaney-stories-1st-dc-letter-column-overstreet-2002-gd/a/13011-15707.s. Accessed 12 January 2021.

Reed, Patrick A. "Celebrating Carl Burgos, Creator of the Original Human Torch." *ComicsAlliance*, 19 April 2016. https://comicsalliance.com/tribute-carl-burgos/.

Riesman, Abraham. "It's Stan Lee's Universe." *Vulture*, 23 February 2016. https://www.vulture.com/2016/02/stan-lees-universe-c-v-r.html.

Rippl, Gabriele, and Lukas Etter. "Intermediality, Transmediality, and Graphic Narrative." In *From Comic Strips to Graphic Novels: Contributions to the Theory and History of Graphic Narrative*, edited by Daniel Stein and Jan-Noël Thon, 191–217. De Gruyter, 2013.

Romita, John, Sr. *Spider-Man Special: "To the Death!,"* 1997. Stan Lee Papers, Box 65, Folder 2.

Romita Sr., John, and Stan Lee. *Spider-Man Special: To the Death!,* 1997. Stan Lee Papers, Box 65, Folder 2.

Russo, Anthony, and Joe Russo. *Avengers: Endgame.* Walt Disney Studios Home Entertainment, 2019.

Salkowitz, Rob. *Comic-Con and the Business of Pop Culture: What the World's Wildest Trade Show Can Tell Us About the Future of Entertainment.* McGraw-Hill, 2012.

Sanderson, Peter. "1940s." In *Marvel Chronicle: A Year by Year History*, 14–43. Dorling Kindersley, 2008.

Siegel, Jerry, and Joe Shuster. *Action Comics* #1. Edited by Vincent A. Sullivan. National Allied Publications, 1938.

Simone, Gail. *Women in Refrigerators*. https://www.lby3.com/wir/. Accessed 22 January 2021.

"Stan Lee." *IMDb*, 5 November 2019. https://www.imdb.com/name/nm0498278 /?ref_=nv_sr_1?ref_=nv_sr_1#actor.

Stan Lee Papers, 1926–2011. https://rmoa.unm.edu/docviewer.php?docId=wyu -aho8302.xml. Accessed 16 November 2019.

Starlin, Jim, et al. *Batman: A Death in the Family*. Titan, 1989.

Stein, Daniel. *Authorizing Superhero Comics: On the Evolution of a Popular Serial Genre*. The Ohio State University Press, 2021.

Stillinger, Jack. *Multiple Authorship and the Myth of Solitary Genius*. Oxford University Press, 1991.

Thielman, Sam. "Goodbye, Alan Moore: The King of Comics Bows Out." *The Guardian*, 18 July 2019. https://www.theguardian.com/books/2019/jul/18 /goodbye-alan-moore-the-king-of-comics-bows-out.

Thomas, Roy, Arvell Jones, and Mike Clark. *All-Star Squadron* #18. DC Comics, 1983.

Tieri, Frank, and Mauricet. *Harley Quinn* #42. DC Comics, 2018.

"Trekkies." *Saturday Night Live*, 1986. https://www.nbc.com/saturday-night-live /video/trekkies/n9511.

"TV Tropes." *TV Tropes*. https://tvtropes.org/. Accessed 19 August 2020.

Walerstein, Mike. 8 December 1972. Stan Lee Papers, Box 12, Folder 3.

Weaver, Tyler. *Comics for Film, Games, and Animation: Using Comics to Construct Your Transmedia Storyworld*. Taylor & Francis, 2013.

Weldon, Glen. *The Caped Crusade: Batman and the Rise of Nerd Culture*. Simon & Schuster Paperbacks, 2017.

White, Ted. "The History of Comics Fandom, Part Three." *Comics Journal*, no. 232 (April 2001): 97–100.

Wickline, Dan. "Writer's Commentary—Gail Simone on Red Sonja/Tarzan #1." *Bleeding Cool*, 2 May 2018. https://bleedingcool.com/comics/writers -commentary-gail-simone-on-red-sonja-tarzan-1/.

Wielgosz, Dave, Paul Kaminski, and Ben Abernathy, eds. *Robin 80th Anniversary 100-Page Super Spectacular*. DC Comics, 2020.

Winick, Judd, Doug Mahnke, Shane Davis, Eric Battle, and Paul Lee. *Batman: Under the Red Hood*. DC Comics, 2011.

Woo, Benjamin. "Readers, Audiences, and Fans." In *Comics Studies: A Guidebook*, edited by Bart Beaty and Charles Hatfield, 113–25. Rutgers University Press, 2020.

Woodard, Jeb, Erika Rothberg, and Alex Galer, eds. *The Joker: 80 Years of the Clown Prince of Crime*. DC Comics, 2020.

Workman, John. 28 October 1998. Stan Lee Papers, Box 106, Folder 13.

Zeck, Mike. *Solarman #2: "This Silent Death, This Hostage Earth" Pencils.* 1989. Stan Lee Papers, Box 57, Folder 4.

INDEX

Page numbers in **bold** refer to tables.

ABOUT THE AUTHOR

Marie Sartain read her first comic book when she was nine years old. Twenty years later at the University of Tulsa, she explored the medium that continues to delight her. When she is not reading her ever-expanding collection of books, Marie can usually be found playing Dungeons and Dragons with her husband in Ohio.